LIBERTY TALES
STORIES AND POEMS INSPIRED
BY
MAGNA CARTA

EDITED BY
CHERRY POTTS

ARACHNE PRESS

First published in UK 2016 by Arachne Press Limited
100 Grierson Road, London SE23 1NX
www.arachnepress.com
© Arachne Press 2016
ISBNs
Print: 978-1-909208-31-5
Mobi/Kindle 978-1-909208-33-9
ePub 978-1-909208-32-2
Edited by Cherry Potts.

Printed on wood-free paper in the UK by TJ International,
Padstow.
*Supported using public funding by the National Lottery through
Arts Council England.*
Images, original Latin text and translation of Magna Carta public
domain, courtesy of the British Library
Photograph page 126 © and by permission of Massachusetts
Historical Society

Individual Copyright

CONTENTS

Introduction: Magna Carta
Cherry Potts

JOHN, by the grace of God King of England, Lord of Ireland, Duke of Normandy and Aquitaine, and Count of Anjou, to his archbishops, bishops, abbots, earls, barons, justices, foresters, sheriffs, stewards, servants, and to all his officials and loyal subjects, Greeting.
TO ALL FREE MEN OF OUR KINGDOM we have granted, for us and our heirs for ever, all the liberties written out below, to have and to keep for them and their heirs, of us and our heirs:

Magna Carta, if you read it, is mainly about asserting the rights and privileges of the higher echelons of society to not be messed about by the king. It has some famous clauses that are still enshrined in law today and some downright wacky ones that don't even translate anymore. Then there are some practical ones which sadly we didn't get stories for: protection of underage heirs, standard measures of wine, ale, corn and cloth, sensible recovery of debt that did not beggar the debtor, restoration of dispossessed lands, including common land, assertion of the ancient liberties of the city of London...

These stories and poems address some specific clauses of Magna Carta but also the more general concept of Liberty. Magna Carta never got as far as freedom, this was liberty for the rich. Serfs had no freedom. Quite a few of the clauses relate to the rights of women. Except that when you read them, they don't amount to a whole hill of beans. Nonetheless we got quite a few stories that address the woman's lot. Pammy in Carolyn Eden's *Free White Towel* would have benefited from the clause on widows' rights, except that she isn't one.

King John has quite a reputation as a bad monarch, and most people have heard of him however inaccurately, either from *Robin Hood, 1066 And All That*, or the wonderful A.A. Milne's poem *King John's Christmas,* and although emphatically *not* about John, the evil king surfaces in several stories.

Some of our stories go that step further, and stray into freedom, of whom to love, the right to roam, to live outside the system, freedom of religious expression, from emotional oppression, and of course, freedom from slavery – all alien concepts to the drafters of Magna Carta.

With the government endlessly flirting with destroying the Human Rights Act, and with no written constitution, even the rights enshrined in Magna Carta can look fragile at times. The fight for liberty isn't going anywhere any time soon.

Where appropriate, I've quoted the relevant clause.

This is the most famous clause of Magna Carta, and one that is still in force.

Nullus liber homo capiatur. vel imprisonetur. aut disseisiatur. aut utlagetur. aut exuletur. aut aliquo modo destruatur. nec super eum ibimus. nec super eum mittemus. nisi per legale judicium parium suorum vel per legem terre.

Nulli vendemus. nulli negabimus. aut differemus rectum aut justiciam.

No free man shall be seized or imprisoned, or stripped of his rights or possessions, or outlawed or exiled, or deprived of his standing in any way, nor will we proceed with force against him, or send others to do so, except by the lawful judgment of his equals or by the law of the land.

To no one will we sell, to no one deny or delay right or justice.

Lag
Jim Cogan

Fry stripped naked while the two of them watched, and then dressed again in the clothes they'd brought on a tray: boxer shorts, socks balled into a lovers' clinch, black jeans that had been almost new on the day he'd arrived. The shirt was as he'd left it. Its freezing fibres billowed round his frame, caricaturing the weight he'd lost. He found his watch shivering in the toe of his left shoe, which rested with its mate atop his jacket.

'Nice,' said Endersby as he watched him shrug the leather on. 'Surprised that one didn't go walkabout.'

There was no mirror, so Fry struck a player's pose and looked at them both with his eyebrows raised.

Hassan obliged with a wolf-whistle.

'Now remember,' said Endersby, 'the magic ends at midnight. If you're not back by then, you'll be leaving your knackers in that tray.'

Hassan smiled. 'He says that to all the girls.'

'Try and be a good boy now.'

'Yes Boss,' Fry grinned and gave them a thumbs-up. They let him out via the air-lock. Sudden oxygen. A drizzle-flecked carpark dotted with staff wheels. It was a short walk to the barrier, past the HMP logo, then a longer trudge to the bus-stop, where a half-dozen day-releasers were already waiting. Grown men with hardened lives and hardened bodies, joshing like teenagers.

After the bus-ride, a railway carriage. Cooling towers looming over the fields. Civilian commuters clutching at their bags, staring at the floor or out of the window, anywhere but at the day-releasers lolling on adjoining seats, their banter ramped up a notch for the occasion, loving the effect they were having on a world that had shut them up for so long.

He sat with the group, keeping silent. An old lady caught his eye. He shook his head and smiled. She looked away, relieved.

An elbow poked his ribs. 'Where you going today, pretty boy?'

It was Gannon. Local lad. Multiple GBH.

'College reunion,' said Fry.

Gannon shook his mangy head and smiled. 'Well I'll be buggered. So am I!'

'Small world,' said Fry.

The pack howled together.

By the time he reached the city centre he was alone, Gannon and the rest having dispersed on the arrivals platform, bound for parts unknown.

The sun was out, filtering down through young leaves, spraying patterns onto the limestone college walls. High walls, built to keep you out, not in. He watched bicycles slipstream each other round a memorial to murdered bishops and thought of Billy MacLeod, the arsonist, with his dewy-eyed nostalgia for the smell of char-grilled human.

The bicycles were piloted by children, children festooned with college colours. Wherever he looked, they were there, the fresh-faced inheritors of his city. His city of speared dreams. Dreams shivved in the prime of life. Dreams running red down a windscreen.

He made his way along the main commercial drag, fighting the tide of bright eyes, youthful smiles and futures still intact. In a small room above a gentlemen's outfitters he sat in a barber's chair, praying for a slip of the blade, then went downstairs to hire a dinner suit. He spent the next two hours alone on a bench by the river, dressed in his finery, his other clothes beside him in a carrier bag as he filled his lungs again and again, trying to stay calm.

When he finally moved, the time on the invitation had long since passed. Ten minutes later he was standing before the studded, weather-beaten gate of his own college, soles teetering on the cobbles, the pointed shadows of the railings reaching across to prod at his heels. The place seemed forbiddingly old-school, nothing like the institution he now called home. More like the Scrubs, or engravings he'd seen of the old Bastille.

Inside, the porter recognised him at once, startling him with the warmth of his greeting. He showed Fry a hatch in the ancient wall where he could leave his rented dinner suit at the end of the night, and promised to see it returned to the shop.

'It's good to see you again,' he said, shaking Fry's hand, and pointed to the glow from the dining hall. Fry could hear cutlery duelling above the evening breeze. His face felt strange, as if a sneeze were on the way.

He walked across the grass. In seventeen years, nothing had changed. Candlelit tables ran the length of the room beneath a high ceiling. Poets, prime ministers and a lone bluestocking saviour of humanity smiled from the panelled walls. Voices purred in an ambience lubed by pre-prandial fizz. Fry paused in the doorway to check the seating plan, even though he'd already received it by post and virtually memorised it in his cell.

Pretending he wasn't *still* checking for *her* name.

Pretending it didn't cause him pain when it *still* wasn't there.

It was a joke, of course. All of it.

A joke that the invitation even reached him in prison. A joke that the screw who opened it had seen fit to pass it straight to the Guv. A joke the Guvnor was probably now telling at parties: his prisoner out on day release to attend a gaudy.

Whatever the ins-and-outs, permission had been granted before he'd even seen the invite. No alcohol, mind, and no staying overnight. The seating plan had arrived a few weeks later.

If her name had been on it he'd never have dared come.

And yet, since it wasn't, what had been the point?

Nothing he ever did made sense.

A couple of diners had noticed him now. A hundred more pairs of eyes might turn towards him at any moment. A last upsurge of pride quelled the urge to run.

Take the plunge. You've done this before.

Just play it like you did on your very first day.

They'd placed him at the end of one of the tables, an empty seat to his left. An ideal vantage point for surveying the room, which he couldn't help doing. Eyes met his and darted away. Hands waved and heads turned, smiling, before swivelling back to ask each other if it was really him.

It took a moment or two to recognise each person. The men were slender boys encased in flesh sarcophagi, familiar eyes, chins and noses protruding through a sea of matter. The women, without exception, were almost too beautiful to look at. Beautiful of face, of body and of attire. He found himself staring at them the way he'd ogled girls as a teenager. The way you'd behold an alien or a goddess.

An old college Fellow sat opposite him. Fry introduced himself.

'Ah. You're the chap who did some time at Her Majesty's pleasure, am I right?'

'Still doing it,' smiled Fry.

The don leant forward with a grin. 'Might I ask what you were in for?'

'Philosophy, Politics and Economics,' said Fry.

The old man, a renowned classicist, pounded the table as he laughed. Fry felt himself relax for the first time since the train.

And then he saw her.

Barely three metres away, at the next table, with her back to him. She turned to speak to the man on her right, lips mouthing in profile. He felt his whole body shudder, heard his mind warble 'What? What?' before it finally clicked, and he started running through the seating plan in his head. He caught her first name, then the duplicated surname shared with the guy who now sat beside her.

Married. To someone they'd both known. Someone *she'd* never stopped knowing.

She seemed taller, rangier. Her hair a different colour.

Maybe.

The rest of the meal was lost on him.

'Done a *Kidman*, hasn't she?'

He'd drunk the coffee but declined the port. The hall was emptying now but still full enough to keep him hidden, and her close by.

He recognised the person who'd slid in beside him, but couldn't remember the name. Another chubby face with too much tooth in the grin.

'A *Kidman*. You know what I mean. Bleached herself, hasn't she? Started out all flame-haired and rosy-cheeked and *ripe*, and now… I mean, what the fuck happened to all those freckles? I'm telling you, I don't even bother watching her films anymore.'

Fry's gaze flitted from the guy's fat hand to the butter knife. The wood of the table was soft enough for a proper crucifixion. That's why all the mess hall surfaces were steel.

She was heading for the exit, her husband's hand in the small of her back.

'Didn't you have a thing with her once?'

'Nicole Kidman? No.'

Fry stood up.

He told himself he'd stay till someone uttered the words 'vehicular manslaughter', but no one did. They made him feel welcome. Valued. Wanted. That made him feel bad. He kept losing her in the crowd, telling himself it was just chance.

When he noticed the clock it was gone eleven, and he knew he'd probably miss his train. He retrieved his carrier bag and got changed in a bathroom. As he stashed the DJ in the porter's hatch he heard his name being called.

She was walking alone by the side of the grass.

'You're not off, are you?'

Fry nodded.

'Jesus, we haven't even… d'you have to? One more drink?'

Her eyes. Full on, like yesterday.

Fry gulped and shook his head. 'I'm on a rather tight schedule. I take it you know about…?'

She nodded. 'Yes. Look, can you wait here? I'll be one minute, that's all. Promise.'

He watched her go. The hair. The shoulders. The calves beneath the hem. He began to panic.

She'd lied. Two full minutes went by before she returned, a car key dangling from her index finger.

'Drive you,' she said.

'Yes, but… are you okay to…?'

'Haven't touched a drop all night.'

Her car was a few streets away, a Volvo four-wheel-drive with a baby seat in the back. She beeped the doors and bade him get in.

'Won't be a second.'

He sat in the front seat looking at the night. He heard the

tailgate open, heard her rummaging in the back, felt the quiver of the suspension as she perched on the bumper. The tailgate slammed, the back door opened and the high heeled shoes she'd been wearing landed in the baby seat. Fry swallowed, unsure whether he could handle the sight of her bare toes flexing on the accelerator. He tried to stop himself from glancing down as she got in, and when he failed he saw she was wearing running shoes, mud-spattered ones with deep rubber lugs, of the type favoured by fell racers.

The engine fired. So did *Adele*. The same song Gannon liked to hum when he did the Times crossword.

Na-na-na-na someone like yoooo-hoo-hoo.

'Sorry,' she said, and killed the stereo.

He hoped he knew why.

They mostly talked about *her*, which felt right. He didn't even need to look at her that much. Instead, he thought of the running shoes, saw her contouring at speed along a muddy incline, soles mauling the turf, her bare legs cased in mud, her breath the only sound against the silence of the hills. As she disappeared behind a crag, he waved good-bye.

When they arrived at the barrier the dashboard clock read 12.07.

He nodded towards the razor wire. 'Quick coffee?'

She answered with a stifled laugh and a grin full of mischief. 'Probably best get back,' she said, and kissed him on the cheek.

He watched the tail-lights disappear and rang the outer bell, getting Hassan on a double shift.

'Tut-tut-tut, Fry. *Very very* tut-tut-tut.'

'Sorry Boss. Won't happen again.'

'I won't tell if you don't. Now get yer jim-jams on and fuck off to bed.'

'Yes Boss,' said Fry, grateful to be home.

Vidua post mortem mariti sui statim et sine difficultate habeat maritagium et hereditatem suam, nec aliquid det pro dote sua, vel pro maritagio suo, vel hereditate sua, quam hereditatem maritus suus et ipsa tenuerint dit obitus ipsius mariti, et maneat in domo mariti sui per quadraginta dies post mortem ipsius, infra quos assignetur ei dos sua.

At her husband's death, a widow may have her marriage portion and inheritance at once and without trouble. She shall pay nothing for her dower, marriage portion, or any inheritance that she and her husband held jointly on the day of his death. She may remain in her husband's house for forty days after his death, and within this period her dower shall be assigned to her.

Free White Towel
Carolyn Eden

I don't miss his breath, stinking of beer and dry roasted peanuts, nor his spittle dribbling on my collarbone, bruised where it wouldn't show.

Now I am an outdoor bird, a magpie watching daybreak's dew, the drizzle of an English summer cooling my healing neck, as the park gates swing open at one or another end of my favourite bus route; the 188 from Greenwich to Russell Square.

I suppose it will be harder when the weather turns.

'Daft cow!' Stanley laughed and I could tell from our chauffeur's wobbling shoulders that he too considered me an object of ridicule.

All I'd said was, 'I didn't know the big sales now start as early as November!' as we cruised along Oxford Street, passing Selfridges and John Lewis still all a-glitter at midnight.

The joke was that I'd mistaken a dismay of rag-bag rough sleepers for bargain hunters.

Why else might someone curl up on the hard ground outside a department store?

Stanley laughing was a bad sign. Too often his chuckles tended to slither into sneers and slaps. I had learnt it was best to say nothing, ask for nothing, for I did indeed need nothing. I belonged beside the Aga while *The City* was Stanley's domain. 'Up West' was not for the likes of me, apart from the annual November hell of a Masonic Ladies' Night.

Ironically it was an overnight Masonic jamboree that gave me the idea. All the wives had a spa session while their other halves bared their calves in ceremonial bonding games. Embarrassed by my lumpen flesh I declined massages and the like but found delight in hiding my flab in the steam room or submerged in the glorious hot tub before huddling beneath a fluffy free white towel upon a lounger. I fell asleep, and when I woke up I thought – I could live like this.

My sleep used to be pocked with anger, fear and worry. The worst dreams were the happy ones, waking from bliss into a bruised chaos that stung like a raw finger dipped into a salt and vinegar packet of crisps I once found abandoned on a memorial bench dedicated to *Robin who so loved it here*.

When I was a child, a meagrely shod, scruffy tramp occasionally knocked on our back door to beg for a glass of water. He'd pilfer whatever lay within a hand's-snatch while mum's back was turned at the sink. He favoured oranges.

Mum taught me that whilst a good deed a day keeps the hubris away, one should never leave a purse on the kitchen table.

I suppose I was lucky to have been brought up in a penny-pinching household where meals were planned to the last splinter of cheddar. Like my mother I have become an obsessive planner. Scrumped apples alone do not make a pie.

I have not yet resorted to stealing although I have been known to 'liberate' some biscuits and ball-point pens from a hotel's amenities trolley.

My incredulity at the vagrants in the big city seems less funny now that I too am homeless.

I was never mighty as in 'look how that mighty Pamela's fallen' but I was certainly a languisher with a body grossly swollen from baked goods munched in solitude.

It was when I started planning that I realised I had no

friends. I'd had nodding acquaintances before our son was exiled to boarding school, but Stanley discouraged close friends. I was hardly 'a lady of leisure-lazybones' like those my mother 'did for'. Maintaining a mansion fit for a mogul was a complex job what with keeping an eye on the cleaners and gardeners and deliveries. Stanley preferred me to personally cook our evening meal and his full English breakfast. Each morning, I would wave him off like a 1950s housewife, swapping his briefcase for a peck on the cheek, hoping he'd have a good day at the office. And I hoped it fervently, because the times his day at the office were less than good, my evenings were bad.

I once overheard Stanley talking to a young man at one of the lodge dinners.

'Take my advice,' Stanley said. 'Find a girl like my Pamela. Plain as a pikestaff with meaty thighs and a docile nature. She'll not cost you a fortune in designer gear, nor be a flirty flibbertigibbet at cricket club teas. You want a wife like a basset hound; loyal, faithful and too fat to run too far!'

Run? *Me?*

The more his bonuses abounded the more I settled into the fog of affluence and accepted gratefully my son sliding away from Stanley's control. Currently James does important work in a Ghanaian medical centre where kindness trumps gold taps and wine cellars. Stanley abhors this altruistic lifestyle. They will not have been in contact. I do email James occasionally from the library and though his replies are curt at least I know he's well.

Where most down-and-outs go wrong is failing to plan. Surely, they must have had some warning and at least a smidgeon of breathing space? Or were they too consumed by hope to admit their sorrows? Or did they just one day snap... turn... walk?

I spent days scheming like a novelist plotting a story

arc. Once I made my decision, recognising the futility of continuing, the thrill of planning took over. My choice was to sink or swim. So I decided to swim – literally.

I've always felt safe in our swimming pool; any swimming pool. As a fat child whose perspiration defeated cheap deodorants, swimming was the only exercise that didn't leave me with the odour of stale sweat. It wasn't so bad at infant school being 'Porky Pammy' but when, after puberty, my nickname changed to 'Stinky Porky Pammy' I took action, and the swimming pool became my sanctuary. So, no doubt to the surprise of my school-mates, I was lithe when Stanley claimed me at the Palais on Ilford High Road.

I'm not a classic hobo. I don't shuffle. I keep my head up and my clothes are not a Guy Fawkes jumble. My flaccid days watching daytime television had educated me into 'cash-converting' and so the proper gold jewellery (albeit given to me by Stanley for appearances) allowed me to pay in cash for my membership and a year's rental on the permanent locker at the health club, so I've no need to trundle my worldly goods around the streets in a shopping trolley.

I reckon that making a leisure club my home (with its inclusive fresh towels) is far better than, say, camping out at an airport, and I found a great deal at a chain motel near Euston; twenty pounds a night if a dozen separate stays were booked in advance. I thus have a room for the first Sunday of each month and Christmas Day. Sheets, duvet and somewhere to properly freshen my clothes – a treat to keep me going. That left me with just under a thousand pounds which equals twenty pounds a week for a year's food.

I spent the last ten nights in the house practising doing without sleep as opposed to not sleeping. Wakefulness is the key to survival. Just as successful tycoons and world leaders are known to function effectively with little sleep, I taught myself to manage with a succession of catnaps. After all, I have neither a country nor a corporation to run.

Only a month after my epiphany in the spa, whilst Stanley was away on a weekend business trip, I left a note on the hall table accompanied by the SIM card from my phone and the low-limit credit card he'd granted me for minor expenses. I left my laptop having first wiped all its history and the emails concerning the hardest of all my planning – acquiring my Freedom Pass; the only way Stanley could trace me, if he could be bothered. I've amazed myself with my talent for deviousness.

Stanley, (the word *dear* not appropriate) *I have left. I want nothing from you. You may divorce me after two years. I repeat: I want nothing but to be rid of you.*

And, reader, I left him. I also left the door of the freezer open – childish I know – and forgot to set the burglar alarms.

Five months, two weeks, four days since I walked… and walked… and then took the bus.

It was more sensible than walking.

I ride the 38 to the British Museum, the 74 to the Victoria and Albert. The 25 goes east, the 171 crosses the river. I adore the 168 to Primrose Hill and sometimes, with only five changes over several hours, I can inhale cockles warming my heart on Brighton beach.

Most of my life is stored in locker twenty-seven within a women's changing room and I am the fittest I've ever been. Arriving at the gym as soon as it opens at six, I catnap in a cubicle for an hour until I hear the cleaner singing her arrival. I shower, rinse my underwear, spinning it in the swim-suit dryer, shaking my knickers beneath the hairdryer. I watch morning television on the recliner bicycle's inbuilt screen and in the early evening I might watch a soap opera or even a documentary as I pound a running machine. I've even been known to swing a few dumbbells. My bingo wings have vanished and a waist unseen for over thirty years now nestles beneath my diminishing bosoms. I swim whenever I want, doze in the steamroom, swelter in the sauna and luxuriate in the jacuzzi. After each shower I wrap myself in a free white towel.

The club has a small café providing free cucumber-flavoured water and daily newspapers. The staff, as in so many establishments, is lackadaisical so I, being a helpful lady, subtly clear tables, sliding edible remnants upon a serviette. If anyone notices, no one cares. The great thing about having dumped one's pride is lack of boundaries. Like the hobo from my childhood I have learnt to pilfer. Today's breakfast was dregs of orange juice, a quarter of a muffin and a barely touched bowl of muesli abandoned by a waif with a ballerina's gait. She'd also left a half slurped milky cup of tea. Bitter tea, nasty tea. I prefer coffee but I am no longer a chooser. Sometimes, I suck on sachets of sugar.

Daytimes, I scavenge throughout the city from St Christopher's Place behind Oxford Street, to the Westfield Malls of Stratford and White City with their vast food courts. I spend a pound a day on a bowl of fruit from Chapel Market, I know where all the best sell-by date offers are, and have developed a nose for those tube stations where free samples are proffered. Last week at Waterloo there were cereal bars and navel oranges promoting the eponymous brand of mobile. I will need fresh shoes soon but have no aversion to rummaging through the charity shops of Kentish Town.

A lady of immaculate appearance will be considered eccentric, not derelict.

The restroom at The Strand Palace (the 91 from Trafalgar Square) has hand cream to splodge where it chafes and Fenwicks has a splendid array of fine fragrances in its powder room, but Harrods is the best for complimentary make-overs, although I make do with any of the others – seventy-two cosmetics counters within a hair's-breadth of Oxford Circus.

I feign interest, wait for the assistant to offer (never ask, too obvious) and hey presto, I am moisturised and painted. I enthuse about all the products but, just as I am about to seal the deal, my phone will thwart the sale.

'Oh no! How awful.' My whisper is tearful. 'I'll be right over… you poor thing!' I thank the assistant and, promising to return, add, 'I do so loathe funerals!'

My skin is bright from the fresh air of night-time walking, my nails are clean and I smell like crushed rose petals.

I have seen the second half of most of the bad shows in Theatreland – and some of the good ones too! Once I picked up a ticket dropped by a gentleman as he dashed into a taxi in Drury Lane only to find myself sat in a Covent Garden box lavished with canapés and wine; the music was quite jolly too.

London has over fourteen hundred hotels – a hundred and eleven designated five-star. Each evening I camp out in a different opulent lounge. My trick is to sink into a comfy armchair in a quiet corner with a library book in one hand and my inert mobile in the other. Should a member of staff approach, I put my phone to my ear as if answering a silent vibrate.

'Darling,' I'll say in a cut-glass accent, 'Oh dear! Don't worry. See you soon.'

Then I smile wanly. 'Just some iced tap water, for the moment, please.'

On good days there are bowls of snacks and sometimes I allow myself to be swept into a wedding or similar buffet-laden function like a maiden aunt everyone half recognises.

The dead time begins when the hotel lounges empty and I lose my invisibility. There's a hotel in Baker Street where the ladies' is tucked away behind small conference rooms barely used in the evenings; so sometimes, when the rain is hard, I sneak a nap there, but mostly I walk or doze on a night bus, my money belt strapped to my skin.

I'm not sure what I will do when my gym membership expires. Other plans bubble including one with a hint of danger. It's what comes of spending evenings in luxurious hotel lobbies, looking ladylike but with a seductive air of elegant wistfulness. Various gentlemen have glanced my way but I've yet to give the nod to their wink.

Alternatively, given my extensive research into the market, I think I'd make a jolly good hotel receptionist.

Bothered
Sarah Evans

Sandra turned the TV on along with her microwave. She reached into her fridge for the half-drunk bottle of white wine. The microwave pinged. The wine sploshed gently into her glass. The news presenter rabbited on.

Election day tomorrow. *Yada, yada*. It had been the only thing in the news for what felt like months. Decades. *Same-old, same-old*. The parties were all the same, give or take, none of them bothered about the likes of her. Why the heck give up her precious time to vote? The current lot told you how everything was getting better. The other lot told you how everything had got worse and they could fix it. No matter who was in power, things were tough then got tougher.

She retrieved a fork, put the microwave meal on a plate and flipped channels to one of the soaps. She settled into the sagging armchair in the corner of the open-plan room. After a day stacking shelves, she was knackered. What did Mr Politician of any colour know about that? Soaps depicted people more like her, people who struggled on low wages and got laid off. People whose relationships broke down and who raised their kids alone.

She put her plate down and poured more wine. The soapland banter seemed a tad boring tonight. Her mind drifted.

Drifted...

She jerked awake. Her skin prickled. It was dark outside and the TV screen glowed green, then white, then purple. Which was odd. Must be a signal problem.

Bleeding nuisance. Might it be time for bed? Yet surely she hadn't slept all evening. She glanced at the clock which usually gleamed at her from the corner. The digits flashed, cycling through nonsense configurations. That was screwed too. Had there been a power outage?

She shivered; she had the unsettling sense of someone watching her. She'd lived on her own since her two girls left for college and being alone had never bothered her. Edge of vision something caught her eye. Her heart beat overtime and she stared determinedly at the TV. *Don't be ridiculous!* She forced herself to turn and look properly. A figure was seated on the high stool at the breakfast bar and was looking down on her.

'Who are you?' she asked. She felt uneasy, yet not as anxious as she ought to do.

The figure was that of a woman, her age indeterminate, her shoulders and half her face draped in some kind of green, white and purple cloak, a gauzy affair that seemed to render the woman translucent.

'I doubt you'd believe me,' the woman said, her voice even and pleasant.

'Try me!' Sandra had come across a lot in her time and prided herself on being worldly-wise and unsurprise-able.

'I'm a ghost,' the woman said and shrugged as if to acknowledge how absurd that sounded. 'The ghost of Liberty hard won.'

'Don't be daft.'

'I said that you wouldn't believe me.'

Sandra was not going to get drawn into this preposterous conversation. 'Would you mind leaving?' she said, the words emerging a little feeble, given an intruder was sitting at her kitchen counter. 'Right now!'

'I'd like to show you some things first,' the woman said.

'What sort of things?' She couldn't believe she was conversing with someone posing as an apparition.

'Come with me and see,' the woman said and held out a hand.

The TV was still cycling green, white and purple. Perhaps

this would be entertaining. *What the hell!*

The woman's hand was cold, but solid, nothing particularly ghost-like about it. Sandra felt a gut-dropping rush, like in a lift or on a fairground ride, a sense of not being firmly rooted to the ground, and she screwed her eyes tightly shut.

Her feet reconnected with something solid.

'You can open your eyes now,' the ghost-woman said.

Sandra found herself dressed in an old-fashioned, long skirt, as was the woman beside her. She couldn't remember when she last wore a skirt; she had certainly never, ever worn a hat, at least not one with a wide straw brim held on by a ribbon. Between the heads of the crowd she could see a race track.

Why would a ghost bother appearing simply to take her to the races? But what would she know about ghost behaviour. If they happened to exist. Which they didn't. *Obviously.*

She inhaled slowly, finding her breathing constricted by a tight, rigid band around her ribs. The air was thick with the smell of old wool and horses and not terribly well washed bodies. She could hear the thunder of hooves and feel the vibration of the earth as the animals turned the bend towards them.

And then...

It all happened so quickly, a blur of confusion. She saw a flash of something white. Heard the snorts of the horses as they reared and swerved in fright. Saw the white slowly turn red.

Dust settled on the scene. The horses stumbled back onto their feet and carried on, one without its rider. People crowded onto the track forming a circle around a body.

Sandra felt a pulse of anger. Why would this woman, ghost, or whatever, take her to the races only for them to witness a violent death. It made no sense.

The crowd buzzed with distress and indignation.

The woman-ghost was looking at Sandra. 'You do know who this is?' she said.

Sandra shook her head; how could she be expected...? But a slow something was creeping in as she remembered a history lesson at school, or some TV drama.

A suffragette had thrown herself in front of a horse, forcing the country's attention on the demand for Votes for Women. *Emily Davison*. The name appeared though she wasn't aware of having known it. The horse thing always sounded so extreme.

'I don't understand,' she said. If this was some kind of electioneering stunt then it seemed rather over the top. It was hard to identify which party this ghost-lady could possibly come from.

The ghost, or whatever she was, looked down at her watch, though it wasn't like anything Sandra had ever seen, the face cluttered with information. Could it be one of those iWatches? A time-travel device? Sandra wanted to giggle. Hadn't ghosts heard of Einstein and relativity? 'It'll have to be a bit of a whistle-stop tour,' the ghost said. 'Hold on.'

They seemed then to zip all over time and place, like in a fast-forwarded film. Images flashed along with snippets of talk. Pompous looking men decreeing that women couldn't be allowed to do this or that, endless claptrap about the weaker sex. Women working in appalling conditions and suffering abuse, dying in childbirth or having their babies taken away. And women – strong and brave – standing up for their beliefs.

Sandra's head was spinning. It came to a pause in some kind of nowhere space.

'Well?' the ghost said.

'Well what?'

'Do you still think you can't be bothered voting?'

'Voting?' Sandra paused. 'I don't see what all that has got to do with voting.'

'No,' the ghost said, sounding a touch impatient. 'But women's suffrage was a key landmark in the slow, hard-won path to female emancipation, alongside all sorts of other rights. To own property, or to divorce. To be educated and have careers. To control fertility or even have access to your own children...' She carried on, ticking things off on her fingers.

'Men had their own battles as well of course...' She stopped. 'But anyway, you'd need my colleague for that. You say things only ever get worse.' Sandra had said that, but not in front of the ghost. 'But over a longer timeframe, you don't have to go back far to see how so many things have got better. Hugely better, actually.'

Sandra still didn't see this had anything to do with the election.

'Imagine taking away women's right to vote,' the ghost continued, as if having read Sandra's thoughts.

'They couldn't do that!' Sandra was hot with indignation.

'Why is it so outrageous to take it away, when you don't plan on using it?' the ghost-lady mused.

'I'm free to use it or not,' Sandra protested.

'True,' the ghost said, in that insufferably reasonable way she had. 'A kind of liberty I suppose. Don't know about you, but I think I've had enough.'

And though Sandra had been feeling that she wanted the evening to be over, now she felt disappointed. The ghost vanished. Sandra was gripped with terror at the thought of being abandoned in some alien time, one in which the choices and independence she took for granted did not apply.

Then everything went green, then white, then purple.

She woke with a stiff neck and throbbing head. She was still in her living room, curled up in the comfy chair, TV blaring out and the clock declaring 07:05.

What a peculiar dream. How odd to have slept all night in the armchair. Except that she felt as if she had not slept at all.

She headed to the bathroom and began to run the shower. She noticed a strange line of bruising around her ribs.

Later, on her way out, she picked her polling card out of the recycling bin. A completely pointless exercise: her single vote would make sod-all difference. She wasn't even sure who she would vote for, though she had some clear ideas on who she would vote against.

She could make her own tiny mark for a Liberty that progressed only slowly, yet gradually accumulated into something more.

If she could be bothered.

The Poppies
Helen Morris

This is Gran's treasure. She takes it carefully out from between the caramel coloured leaves of the book, very carefully. The book is 'The Water Babies' by Charles Kingsley. The bright cornflower blue cover woven tightly, but you can still see the weft and weave of the fabric. There are indents where it was once embossed with gold print, but now worn back to the cover, the pages crisp and stiff, holding hard on to their memories and their treasures, stiffening as age stiffens us all. Gran keeps the photo there because that's where she first tucked it, all those years ago, when the pages were pliable. As were Gran's fingers, which are now bent, with skin soft and folded. But still, she handles the photo so gently: a treasured memory, held as if it were the thinnest blown glass. The photo is bronze sepia. It seems sun-bleached. But it's just age – no sunlight reaches it in the pages of the book. Time has reached in its fingers and taken the photo's definition as it takes life. Slowly. Surreptitiously. Silently.

She brushes imaginary dust from the photo with the side of her hand. It's really a caress, full of its own dust. Then she places it flat on the table between us. Some of her grey white hair has come lose, drifting spiders' webs caught in a shaft of sunlight. She wears her hair in two long plaits, folded across the top of her head and pinned with long crooked hairpins that tinkle to the floor when she walks. She's as slight and frail as thistle down, and as stubborn and impossible to shift as a bramble and bracken-clenched farm gate.

We look at the photo, still bursting with life even after seventy years.

Gran smiles. She breathes in, and her sparrow-bone shoulders straighten. 'Hardly twenty the both,' she says. The photo is slightly out of focus and I move closer to peer at the two women who look back at me. Not much older than me, but from a time when you grew faster and lived more precariously.

'Poppy Smith and Poppy Miller', says Gran. 'The Poppies, as they were known. That one, that's Poppy Smith.' I look – she has her chin up, looking confidently at the camera. 'Probably checking out the cameraman.' Gran says. 'You can't tell, because it's black and white, but her hair was a beautiful chestnut. Like a newly skinned conker. She had mischief running through her like a stick of rock.'

I wait, and Gran goes on. 'She stole a motorbike from the farmer's barn once and rode it cool as a cucumber down to the village shop. Lord knows how she knew how to drive it. She looked like an Amazon warrior. Proud, beautiful.'

Gran pauses. She takes a sip of her tea. I made it. She doesn't approve of the fact I use tea bags. So much so that I have to bring my own because she won't have them in the house. She won't have them. Not in her white and green tiled kitchen as cool as the bottom of the sea. But I'm not messing with loose leaf. It's like the dregs in the bottom of a vase of flowers left too long and gone crispy, I tell her. Like dried love. But of course she does it her way when I'm not around. With loose leaf, a teapot, a tea cosy and a tea strainer. Properly.

'Poppy Smith came from Bradford,' says Gran. 'She'd been working in a laundry. When she spoke it felt like a punch. She spoke straight to everyone. Even Mr Bennett the farmer. We used to catch our breath with the nerve of her. But she had charm as well as cheek. She got away with it. Being with her was like walking a knife edge. But she had a great heart in her too. There was a book of fairytales in one of the rooms, I remember. She'd never heard them before. "Not much time for books and fairytales in Bradford," she said. She loved them. I found her crying over Cinderella once. We clung on to things like that. Good triumphing over evil, happily ever after. We needed hope in the face of the Nazis. We didn't care how real that hope was.'

I look at Poppy Smith. I wonder how it was to be lifted out of a laundry in 1940s Bradford and moved hundreds of miles to a farm in rural Berkshire at barely 20. I wonder if she was scared. Or excited. Or maybe both.

'That's Poppy Miller,' Gran says nudging with her middle knuckles the other girl, her fingers too curled now to stretch out and point. Poppy Miller is smaller and darker. Her curls hanging forward over her face, a more reticent grin. 'Not as full on as Poppy S, is she? But maybe she knew the cameraman wasn't looking at her face.' Gran grins. 'She filled those dungarees better than any other girl on the farm.'

'Gran!' I say. And she chuckles. She likes to shock me. Last week's visit she said 'Wanker' and 'Fuck Off' with such force about a man in the village that I nearly inhaled my gingersnap. He was spouting anti-immigration stuff at community coffee. Gran has no truck with that kind. She lives on the spot where she was born. She told him there and then that if he believed people should go back to where they came from he should fuck back off to Maidstone. She'd seen what nationalism does. She knows the evil it breeds and nurtures. The knife blade it twists and splits. The lies, the forked tongues.

But now she's back on the story. I'm letting her talk. A few years ago I'd have been bored, but not now, now I want to hear.

'Poppy Miller came from Barnsley,' says Gran. 'She was

softly spoken and her vowels rolled like warm boiled potatoes in a pan. She'd been working washing bottles in a glass factory. Great red raw hands from the heat of the water. Nerves in the end of her fingers dead. When she came here she tried to keep her hands hidden. But there are no physical secrets when you're living cheek by jowl like we were. She had a lovely singing voice. Soft, but with something, broken. She'd sing us folk songs. Galway Shawl was my favourite.'

'They'd never known such freedom as when they became Land Girls. Suddenly whisked away from their oppressive suffocating dark cities. Their lives were mapped out: factory jobs, or an office job if they were lucky; then marriage – to men who wouldn't appreciate them. Being here was like a fairytale from the book to them. They never went back. The land broke them free. Even though it was hard and dirty, even though they'd never seen a cow and wouldn't go near one for the first week, even though they got cold as cold and wet as a pond dipper. I didn't understand at the time, I was born and raised on the farm, didn't question it, but in those years we learned to be ourselves and not look to a man to define who we were. That was new. That was something the war gave us.'

'Bloody hell Gran,' I say. 'I thought feminism was the sixties.' Gran laughs and her face crinkles up like a brown paper bag, and her chest wheezes.

'If we'd have had the pill we'd have been unstoppable,' she says, 'but that wasn't for another twenty years and too late for us. But we made our own liberation the best way we could. Not like you young woman nowadays creating, prisons for yourselves when you've got all this freedom to grab.'

I think about Kim Kardasian's arse photos and I wonder where we got so lost. 'Maybe we're too safe, Gran,' I say. 'Maybe you need a war to really understand freedom? Maybe we take our liberty for granted?'

I wonder what the Poppies would be like if they were young today? I look back down at the photo. Would they be whitening their teeth and darkening their lashes? Stripping the hair off their bodies and volumising the hair on their heads? Would they be wearing push up bras and tummy control knickers? Would they be looking at celeb cellulite online?

Gran looks at me. 'Liberation is not something you win once,' she says. 'It's a battle that goes on. You can't get complacent... Look at us getting all heavyweight,' she says and she leans back over the photo.

'See. They've been stacking hay. A traditional haystack, not these machine rolled sausage things or square bales you get nowadays. A proper haystack – for finding needles – or rolling in with young men. You couldn't do that on a modern one, no give in it, though you'd still get sharp stalks in your backside. They're using pitchforks. You could do a lot of damage with a badly swung pitchfork. They take strength and control to use. They learnt quickly, those two. They saw an opportunity, and they embraced their strength, their grace. They made a good team.'

I get the biscuit tin down. Half a cup of tea. Then a biscuit. I know the routine now. A barrel biscuit tin, covered with pictures of what I think are supposed to be British wild flowers, but drawn by someone, in a factory far across the world, who has never seen one.

'The Poppies,' says Gran, 'were the most vibrant and alive thing on that farm. You couldn't work after dark, not like now. No lights. We'd sit talking around the fire. The stories they told! Oh my! I wouldn't repeat them for fear my hair would stand on end. I lost touch with them when they left. Two months after peace was declared, that would have been. I don't know where they went – they were just off. They left together; on the bus, laughing, of course. The photographer – he brought the photo back round – he only just missed them. Gave it to me, asked me to pass it on, but of course – I never did get a forwarding address, so here it still is.'

'I could look for them, Gran,' I say. 'There's Facebook now, and Google.'

She pauses and in that heartbeat I feel both the sharpness of loss and the acceptance with which the years have smoothed it.

'No. No, I want to remember them like this. That day. That August day. It was hotter than an oven. I don't want to see two old women like me. Maybe even two dead women. This is them. The Poppies. This is the way they stay.'

And she reaches in the tin for a hobnob and slides the photo gently back into the front cover of the book.

Safe.

Her treasure.

Liber homo non amercietur pro parvo delicto. nisi secundum modum delicti: et pro magno delicto amercietur secundum magnitudinem delicti. salvo contenemento suo.

For a trivial offence, a free man shall be fined only in proportion to the degree of his offence, and for a serious offence correspondingly, but not so heavily as to deprive him of his livelihood.

Stopped by a Busker
Owen Townend

The busker has trimmed curls beneath a flat cap, a van dyke, piercings in a downward-facing triangular formation, and a black violin.

A man with orange headphones hassles him.

I get close. The man with the headphones just wants to know why the busker doesn't record his talents. The busker smiles impatiently and explains that that's just *not his thing*.

I throw some coins into his case, tell him that he's doing just fine in my opinion.

'Hey,' he says, 'How are you?'

'I'm fine thanks,' I say, seeing the baby-faced student I grew up with behind all the studs and fancy facial hair. 'And you, Curt?'

The orange headphones are back over the defeated stranger's ears and he mumbles away from us.

Apparently Curt has left home and is now living with his girlfriend, splitting shifts at a local vegan cafe.

I work part-time too, but I'm still living at home. He obviously doesn't understand this, but he doesn't judge either.

He tunes up his violin and tells me that he's recently been arrested and that's why his name might come up online. He was protesting up and down Friendly Street, a demonstration against the new immigration laws. His girlfriend was arrested too but her parents got them both out. They *get it*, apparently.

'Do you have any requests?' Curt asks.

I joke '*In the Air Tonight* by Phil Collins? The drum solo. A bit of a challenge for you.'

'I meant classical music, and, anyway, Collins is crap.'

'I quite like *Invisible Touch*.' I say, then remember that isn't actually Collins.

He plays a summery tune for a summery day. I look down at his case, the coins he's collected. More silver than copper with a few glints of gold.

'You take care.'

He pauses his bowing to wave goodbye. A well-dressed stranger drops some more money into his case. Another follows suit.

I'm back in the crowd, heading down to the shopping mall. Those tiled floors don't just clean themselves.

Curt is fiddling away. I can still hear his music at the revolving doors.

Lucky busking, I think. *You son of a bitch.*

I've since tried to looked him up online – but, of course, he's changed his name.

Omnis kidelli de cetero deponantur penitus de Tamisia, et de Medewaye, et per totam Angliam, nisi per costeram maris.

All fish-weirs shall be removed from the Thames, the Medway, and throughout the whole of England, except on the sea coast.

Into The Blue
Nick Rawlinson

'Will you look at that,' Bennett's granddad said. We had crossed the big field and were now, at last, next to the river. The grass around us was thick with cowpats, and on the opposite bank, rows of willow trees were bent over to admire themselves in the water. But Bennett's granddad wasn't looking at them. His head was tilted so far back I thought he might fall over. He was looking straight up.

'That's lovely,' his granddad said. 'Isn't that lovely, lads? Now, what colour would you say that was?'

Bennett frowned. 'It's the sky, grandad,' he said. 'It's blue.'

'Yes,' the old man said. Bennett was about to walk off again, but his granddad didn't move. 'What kind of blue, though?'

Bennett looked at me and shrugged. 'Sky blue,' he said. 'Can we go fishing now?'

Bennett was carrying the tackle box and the rods. I was carrying the net, but Bennett's granddad still didn't move. Instead he turned to me. 'What do you think, Richard?'

Bennett was my best mate, but I liked his granddad. This walk was his idea. He'd got us out of a double English lesson. So I looked up too.

The sun was warm on my face. I could see the sky.

'It's…' I said.

'Blue?' he chuckled.

'Well – yeah.'

'You sure?'

I looked again. 'There are clouds,' I said. There were, too. Big, white, fluffy ones, the sort you only get on sunny afternoons.

'Fat as abbots, serene as swans,' Bennett's granddad said. 'Anything else?'

I stared. That's when the funny feeling started. Like I'd never looked at the sky before. Not properly, I mean.

It's – it's not all the same, is it?' I said. 'The blue. At the bottom – I mean, near the trees, the horizon whatever – it's lighter than it is up – up there.'

'That blue,' Bennett's granddad said, quietly, 'is the colour of a Spitfire pilot's shirt. And of Shakespeare's eyes. And the Artful Dodger's coat.'

'Don't be daft,' Bennett said. 'His coat was grey.'

I looked at Bennett, surprised.

He looked at me, like I was three and a bit stupid. 'Artful Dodger. Me Auntie Steph's dog? The rescued greyhound, used to bite your legs. Remember? '

I did. That dog would chase me for hours. Round and round the scrubby allotment Bennett's family called 'the Land'. They never grew anything there. It was too covered in rubbish, old bricks and that, and there were more nettles than you could slash with a stick. But there was also this stream, where we could build bridges and throw stones and do whatever we liked. Provided we kept an eye out for the dog poo.

'That colour,' Bennett's granddad said, 'has been over people's heads since, well, before there were people. It was there when the Romans invaded, and the Normans. When William Blake walked this green and pleasant land.' He looked at me. 'You look at the sky, you look at history. It's seen so much, that blue. Holds it all.' He looked up again. 'If only we could read it, what we'd know.'

Bennett slapped me on the stomach.

'Can we go now?' he said. 'I want to fish.'

'Ah,' Bennett's granddad said. 'Well...'

'What?' Bennett said.

His granddad looked a bit shifty. 'I told Mr Thomas I was going to give you a history lesson, so I really ought to...'

'Uh,' Bennett said.

'Come on, now, lads. He gave you the afternoon off...'

'Tommo won't care,' Bennett said.

'I think you're being a bit unfair,' his granddad said.

Bennett snorted. 'Tommo gives the afternoon off to anyone who wants it.' He looked at me and grinned. 'He's glad to get rid of us.'

'Oh, surely not,' his granddad said.

''Course he is. He just has to pretend he isn't. He has these targets, yeah? Truancy and that. But as long as you say, "Mr Thomas, it's for a learning objective" or, "it's part of my family's culture", then he's all too happy.'

I looked at Bennett's granddad. He seemed kind of crumpled. I felt bad. I could feel my face colouring.

'But,' I said.

Bennett scowled at me. But I couldn't stop myself.

'We'd really like to know, wouldn't we, Bennett. About what you want to tell us, about history and – and that,' I said.

'Really?' Bennett's granddad said. 'Well, I s'pose. While we're here. I mean, it's not every day you get to see something as important as this.'

'Thanks, Dick,' Bennett said.

I looked at his granddad. 'So?' I said.

'Oh,' his granddad said, 'right.' He walked to the edge of the river, peered upstream, downstream, then nodded. 'Yes. I thought so. Well, we're here.'

'Finally,' Bennett said. He knelt down and opened the

tackle box, and began selecting a float, pinching together lead shot beneath his stubby fingers.

'So, do you see it?' Bennett's granddad nodded at the river.

'What?' I said.

'That. There.'

'Um.' I followed his gaze. But there was only the slow shift of the river, and the flickering silver-blue dance of the reflected sky. 'I don't see – anything.'

Bennett's granddad grinned wildly, like I'd said exactly the right thing.

'Yes,' he said, 'that's the point.'

'Wait,' Bennett said. 'You mean we just walked a mile across a bloody field to look at something that isn't here?'

'Language, lad,' his granddad said. 'Although you're right, in a way. Blood may have been spilled here, because of that.' He nodded again.

'Something that isn't here,' I said.

'Exactly,' he said. Then, when he'd held the moment as long as he could without looking weird – weirder, at least – he rubbed his hands together and chuckled.

'As far as I can make out from local records, this used to be the site of a fish weir.'

'A what?' I said.

'It was a trap. Designed to catch fish. About 800 years ago, there would have been a great 'V' across the river, made out of stones and wooden posts. It would've stretched from here to about…' – he peered at the opposite bank – '…there, d'you see? Next to that tree that's a bit collapsed into the water. The tip of the V was left open, you see, and they'd put a basket woven out of reeds or hazel in the gap. Any fish heading downstream would be funnelled into it. The basket was kind of a double ice cream cone, one bit inside the other. Easy for fish to swim into, hard to get out.'

'How many fish?' Bennett asked.

'Maybe hundreds at a time,' said his granddad. 'Congers, roach, pike, chub. They'd have to stand here on the bank, to pull the basket in with ropes.'

Bennett looked at the river.

His granddad sat down and started taking off his shoes and socks.

'What are you doing?' Bennett said.

'I,' said the old man, 'am going paddling, to see if I can find any remains.'

'But won't it've, like, washed away?' I said.

'Oh no. Oak is very durable. There's remains of these traps all up and down the river.'

'But you can't go in,' Bennett said.

'It's alright, lad, I won't go very deep.'

'No, I mean you'll scare the fish!'

'Oh,' the old man said. 'I see. Oh. Well, we don't want that. Maybe I'll just dip me toes in. Cool them down a bit.'

'Don't! I mean it! You'll splash.'

'I won't...! I won't splash.'

'You'll splash!'

'When,' I said, then swallowed, tried to think what to say next, 'I mean, how did you find out about it? The weir?'

Bennett's granddad looked at Bennett, then dipped his toes, gently, into the water. 'See? No splash. Documents, Richard,' he said. 'In the library. So old, they're as brown and fragile as moths' wings. If you touch them, they disintegrate so bad there's nothing left but a stain on your fingers.'

I looked at the river again. I didn't know what to say.

A bird started singing somewhere.

'I was researching,' Bennett's granddad said. 'Into Magna Carta. You'll have been hearing all about that at school, I expect, what with the anniversary and all.'

'Er,' I said.

Bennett's granddad frowned. 'You must've been.'

I shook my head. 'Not really.'

'Not ...? But it's history. British history. Your heritage.'

'Mr Thomas says there's no such thing as history,' I said.

'No such ...?! Of course there's history. You're surrounded by it! It's here!'

'Or not here,' I said.

'There are facts. Runnymede, King John, the Barons' War!'

'Tommo,' Bennett said, 'says historical facts are only the propaganda of the dominant discourse. What we call history is merely a subjective interpretation, distorted by the contemporary, er, diet-something.'

'Dialectic,' I said.

'Yeah,' Bennett said, 'that's it. Diabetic.'

'But,' Bennett's granddad said, '1215 is one of the most important dates in human history!'

'Tommo says there's no point learning dates, only having opinions,' Bennett said.

'Is that what passes for teaching nowadays? Having opinions?'

'He says the old-fashioned rote-learning of so-called history only discriminates against those without a facility for – you know. Recall.'

Bennett's granddad snorted. 'Facts are the map of the past, lad, that help us navigate the future. Magna Carta is the greatest gift Britain ever gave the world. He must've said something about it.'

I looked at Bennett. 'Well...' I said.

Tommo had tried. In class he'd said, 'What's your opinion of Magna Carta?' And to everyone's surprise, Bennett put up his hand. 'Yes Bennett?' 'I don't like it, sir.' 'Why ever not?' 'I don't like the chocolate on these new Magnums, sir. I prefer

Feasts,' and everyone had laughed and although Tommo'd said 'MagNA not MagNUM' and 'Alright, settle down' about a hundred times, we all knew the lesson was finished.

'It was,' Bennett's granddad said, 'a bill of rights. It didn't work straightaway. They needed several more versions of it, but it established that there were such things as rights, and liberty. It was the basis for loads that we now take for granted. Parliament. Trial by jury. The American constitution. Individual freedom.'

'My mum,' said Bennett. We stared at him. 'Well, she says my dad's always taking her for granted.'

'But what's a fish weir that's no longer here got to do with Magna Carta?' I said.

'In 1215,' Bennett's granddad said, 'according to the church, for nearly six months of the year the only thing you were allowed to eat was fish. And if you were poor, that was all you could afford anyway. So there was a clause in Magna Carta that said all fish weirs had to be removed.'

'I don't get it,' I said. 'If it was so good for catching fish, why'd they want to take it down?'

'Because trapping all the fish here means everyone downstream goes hungry. Plus, boats couldn't get past them, see? It was only a little thing. But it established a right. The right to free movement. For fish, for boats, for the river.'

I looked at Bennett's float, bobbing on the water. It was almost hidden in the sparkles on the surface. We all watched it for a bit, waiting for that telltale wobble that would mean a bite.

'Why?' I said.

'Well.' Bennett's granddad dusted his hands on his trousers. 'King John and the Barons were at war…'

'No,' I said, 'I mean, why are you telling us? About the fish weir? It's not like we have an exam on it or anything.'

Bennett's granddad looked at me. 'Ideas have to be treasured, Richard. Passed on. So they're not forgotten.

Submerged you might say. Do you see?'

'Not really,' I said.

'Oh, for god's sake, you two,' Bennett said. 'Can't I fish in peace?'

I looked at Bennett's granddad, expecting him to answer. But he just lay down and closed his eyes. I looked at Bennett, but the float was dancing. He'd got a bite.

So I did the only thing I could think of. I lay down too. And I looked up.

Into the blue.

Omnes obsides statim reddemus

We will at once return all hostages.

The King's Computer
Liam Hogan

If you tip water into my mouth, I will drink. If you place a morsel of food in my mouth, I will chew, and swallow. These are involuntary actions, necessary, but of no importance. They do not distract me from my purpose, which is to think.

I was trained from an early age to perform this function. Trained to memorise, to calculate, and to compute. My brain has been honed into a perfect machine, dedicated to solving the King's problems, however banal.

I do not need light to think, so I sit in the dark. I do not need soft beds, or fresh air, or companionship. I do not need music, or art, or laughter. I avoid these distractions by operating in a room deep under the castle. Once it was a wine cellar: it is dark, and it stays the same temperature all year round. The single entrance is kept locked, and only those with legitimate access to me are permitted to enter. The only other similar location for me – the dungeons – are noisy and chaotic by comparison.

I do not sleep while I am thinking – I am trained to rest different parts of my brain at a time, so that I can keep a chain of thought alive. But when I have no problems to solve, I do little except sleep. This allows me to build new connections between the data and conclusions I have made, and helps me to better tackle future problems.

I woke from such a sleep as the door of my room creaked open. A light approached, merely a candle in a pewter holder, but painfully bright to my sensitive eyes. I quickly ran through the mental exercises I perform upon every awakening; they sharpen the mind, ready to accept a new challenge.

I did not recognise the girl who stood uncertainly before me.

'Are you the King's Computer?' she asked, in a lilting, foreign, accent.

'I am,' I confirmed.

'And you can answer any question?'

'No,' I replied. I could have left it at that, but if I have a fault, it is pride in my abilities, so I explained to her why her question was wrong. 'I am not omniscient. Some questions require information I do not have, and so I must ask for that information before I can answer.'

She nodded. 'What is love?'

I paused. It was not the sort of question I was asked. I ran through what data I had.

Love is a many splendoured thing.

Love is blind.

All you need is love.

I stared at her, and she held my gaze unabashed. 'That is your question? What is love?'

'Yes. What is love? How long does love last? And how do you know when you are in love?'

'I will need to think about this,' I said.

She gently inclined her head, and turned to go. 'Wait,' I commanded. 'I need to know what level of priority this question has, in case other demands are made of me.'

She brought the candle closer to her other hand, and I saw the oversized signet ring that her slim finger bore, and as she left I settled into my thoughts.

She returned twelve hours and thirty-four minutes later.

'How are you getting on?' she asked.

I paused a moment before answering, uncertain what to say. 'It's a tricky one.'

'Yes.' she nodded. 'Do you need anything? Any input?'

I had not rung the bell. There was nothing I knew for certain that I needed. But she was offering me information. 'I need to know the average dowry of a farm girl. The number of silk favours displayed during the last Michaelmas joust. The number of apothecaries on Downham Row last year, and now.'

She laughed, a light musical laugh. 'Very well. I shall try and find out for you. Anything else?'

'I need to know what chocolate tastes like,' I stammered. 'I need to know what wind feels like as it brushes through your hair on a warm summer's day. I need...' I did not know what else I needed.

She looked up at me pityingly. 'You do not know these things? Oh the evil of it! But now I hear someone coming, so I must go.'

She slipped into the corridor beyond the door and I heard muffled voices, coarse laughter, a shriek, the sharp retort of a slap. The door opened again and two of the Advisor's clerks bounced into the room.

'My, that's a mighty fine piece of ass!' one said as he rubbed his reddened cheek. 'I wouldn't mind being the King for a day – I'd return her little love tap in spades!'

'Jack, you don't half pick 'em.' the other said wearily, as he laid a few scrolls on a desk by the door. 'If it ain't the nearest gutter-wench it's a mountain princess who'd fillet you before she'd give you the time of day!'

'Whatd'ya mean? She's a mere slip of a girl. Feisty, but give me a couple of hours and I'd have her eating out of me hands.'

The one who was not Jack scoffed. 'She's more likely to serve your hands to you for dinner. I hear that where she's from the lady-folk keep wickedly sharp daggers in their pants. The King won't let her near him until she's been thoroughly strip-searched. Now THAT I would like to see! What was she doing in here?'

Jack shrugged. 'Beats me. I wouldn't want to spend any more time down here than I have to. Gives me the creeps. Shall we get on?'

They asked me a dozen petty questions about the state of the Armoury and the number of Men At Arms that could be levied by the Kings' Dukes. I refused to answer, telling them that they would have to wait. They called the Advisor, who shouted at me, and threatened to deprive me of food, but to no avail. So he called the General.

'So what's all this?' the General barked. 'Bloody Advisor messing with your head again? He shouldn't be allowed to look after someone as valuable as you, my boy! But we've work to do, so let's have no more nonsense. The mountain tribes are amassing on our borders, come to rescue their damned princess. They're unruly, but numerous – never seen so many of the blighters! So we need to come up with a plan...'

'I am already working on a question.' I interrupted.

He laughed, a deep booming noise in the small confined space. 'Never mind that, my lad. Here's my ring, so clear the decks! Now their army is 20,000 strong...'

'The question I am working on takes priority,' I told him.

He stopped, and then turned and stared at the Advisor, who blanched. 'I know nothing, General Sir. But the only person with higher authority than you is the King.'

The General drummed his fingers on the pommel of his sword.

'Well,' he said quietly. 'If the King...' and then he abruptly spun on his heel and marched out.

I ignored the harsh words of the Advisor, and when he

began slapping me and stars appeared before my eyes, I ignored those as well, and eventually he too left.

She returned as promised, eleven hours and thirteen minutes later. All day long I had heard construction noises in and around the castle, and I wanted to ask her what all the commotion was. But it was not pertinent to the problem.

She told me what she'd learnt about the dowry, the favours, and the chemists, though none of it was important anymore, as my calculations had moved on from there. And then she stood on her tiptoes and pressed something between my lips. An intense burst of bitter flavour flooded my mouth. I rolled the slowly melting ball around, feeling it coat my tongue and my teeth.

'That,' she said 'is chocolate. The best there is. None of this valley rubbish.'

I swallowed hastily. 'I did not need to taste it. I merely needed you to describe it to me.'

She laughed again, the same lyrical laugh. 'Some things can't be described. Like this...'

She bent forward, raised the candle, and gently blew. Warm air spilled over my bare arms, and the hairs twitched and then stood upright. I looked down in wonder.

'So,' she asked quietly. 'Do you know the answer yet?'

'No,' I admitted. 'But... I know what it is not.'

'Oh?' she said, her eyes twinkling in the candlelight.

'It is not oysters, or powdered rhino horn, or any other aphrodisiac. It is not a magical enchantment, or chemical potion.'

'All true,' she said. 'But not the answer.'

'No,' I agreed, emboldened. 'I know also that it cannot be imprisoned, or forced. It is not a matter of convenience; it cannot be arranged, bartered, or planned for. And it does not know rank, or race.'

'You're getting closer,' she said, smiling, and I felt warmth at her words. 'But I think you need some more inspiration.'

She took a sponge from a leather bag and mopped my brow, the coolness of the water startling me. She crushed lavender in her petite hands, the smell infused the air, briefly banishing the stale mustiness. And she danced for me, her shadow cast by the solitary candle weaving itself into my consciousness.

'Why do you spend so much time with me?' I asked.

'Because I want to.' was her simple reply. 'And because only in your cell am I not treated as a prisoner.' She stopped her swaying, and drew a delicate finger over my cheek and lips. 'Ahh, I wish I could spend more time with you. But I will be missed, however chaotic it is up there, and when they come looking, they must not find me here. So farewell, King's Computer.'

I... I lost track of time. Something I had not done since I was a child, forced to count the grains of sand in a thimble, while declaiming in Greek. All I could think of was the touch of her hand.

So I don't know exactly when it was that the King stormed in. 'They tell me – God! It stinks down here!' He stopped abruptly and turned on the Advisor. 'You loathsome reptiles, do you never give him a wash? At least someone has had the sense to strew lavender.' He waved his nosegay under his nose. 'So, you won't take orders from anyone but me. Well here I am, and here's the situation. The General rode out to meet the advancing army last night, and was soundly defeated. He told me you'd given him an unbeatable strategy, whereas the Advisor says you did nothing of the sort. Damned fool! It's a good thing he's dead, otherwise I'd be wearing his hide right now! The heathen rabble advance on, dammit! I won't rest until their whole army fertilises my fields.' He paused. 'Which is the problem. Only a few of my army made it back. We're prepared for a long siege, but I've no intention of spending the rest of winter a prisoner in my own kingdom! So, compute. We have a dozen trebuchets, a bit short on ammo for them, and half a dozen siege machines. Not sure what use they will be, but...'

'I have an answer.'

The King stopped mid-word. A smile exploded across his bearded face. 'I KNEW it! Never let me down yet! So, what's the plan?'

'First release the mountain princess. Send her with a small escort to meet the approaching army.'

His face turned red, his meaty hands formed fists. And then he slowly relaxed. 'Well. There are plenty more where she came from, especially if it will secure the destruction of their whole army...' He turned and snapped orders to his Captain of Arms, who departed rapidly up the stairs.

'And next?' he asked eagerly.

'Throw open the castle gates. Better yet, sever them from their chains, and allow them to fall into the moat.'

He smiled. 'Ahh. I see a ruse coming. A master stroke, yes? A feint – the castle becomes a steely trap? Cunning! Very cunning. Where's the Captain, ah blast it. Advisor, see that it is done!'

The Advisor nervously adjusted his cloak. 'But sir...'

'Now goddammit, or I'll be wearing your hide instead!' the King roared, and the Advisor fled.

'And the final part?' the King asked, breathlessly, now that we were alone.

I calculated. The Captain would take time to select the escort, uncertain how well the mountain tribes would treat them. And the Advisor would need to call upon armed guards to convince the Gate Master to do as he told him. But none of that mattered, because the Advisor in his haste had slammed the cellar door shut, and it only opened from the outside. I waited a moment until he was out of earshot.

'Love is putting someone else before yourself. Love is forever. And you know when you are in love only if you are in love.'

And then I stared down at the crushed lavender and awaited my fate.

Jail Break

Kate Foley

on not speaking enough Dutch

I have made a little prison for myself.
Outside, words fall from the trees
like apples.

The newsreader folds his face
in planes of sorrow. Who
is being carried out in that black bag?

Not everything is hidden.
There is always the language of lips
that conjugates harmony

of bed and table
and a language of hands
where tenderness lies in the stroke

of the fine hairs
on our separate skins.
But isn't it time for a jail break?

Shall I pray to myself to find my legs?
To let myself out? I won't shoot my jailer –
we've known each other far too long –

no. We'll join hands and run
like rabbits over the free grass
that speaks in tongues

and shout irregular verbs.

Cena
Peter DeVille
(*After Martial*)

Enzo, Aldo, Piera, Pippa, are you coming for a meal?
The table's for six, I'll add a chair, call Daniel.
Claudia brought some mallow leaves to help digestion
And there's tons of green stuff from the garden,
Lettuce, big crisp leaves, and onions chip-and-chopped,
There's mint to make you belch, and the herb that gets
you horny,
Fresh mackerel with sliced eggs, tomatoes, peas,
Slivers of anchovy, salmon to break open too.

That's all *hors d'oeuvre*: my dinner's little with a big plate:
A piglet Tanzo got from somewhere, mum's the word,
So succulent you won't need knives, perhaps no forks.
There's broad beans, Brussels sprouts (the little ones)
And a chicken, and a leg – what's left – of seasoned ham
Big enough to regal forth on two or three occasions.

To finish you off, there's fresh figs, apples, oranges, pears
And a honeyed wine that curls about the tongue.
I'll give you some: we'll have jokes without nastiness,
Free talk that we won't have to fear tomorrow.
My guests can talk of Milan, Bolton, Arsenal.
My pints of wine won't send anyone to jail.

Girl in a Suitcase
Cassandra Passarelli

The sky's a bowl with a lid of clouds. Palop is close to the brim: some days our heads touch heaven. During rainy season, when our streets turn into rivers of thick red mud, the lid is tightly shut. In winter, fog descends at midday and no one leaves their house. In November the sun breaks through, hardening the mud, warming skin and drying clothes. Then we smile easily, wash our hair and visit neighbours. I am called Jacinta after my uncle, Jacinto. He disappeared north, along the mule path that leads to Mexico and the world, before I was a twinkle in Mami's eye. He returned from Florida when I was in nappies with stories of slave-driving gringos and thieving Negroes. And a grey vinyl suitcase full of gifts. He didn't bring me anything – didn't know I'd been born. So he gave me the suitcase.

Our yard is full of creatures. Elena the Elder is known for her sharp tongue. My hairball puppy, Sochi, chases the squawking chicken, head lowered. Jacinta the Elder married and has five of her own. The turkey chases Sochi. Cecilia left for Washington three years ago. The black sow, tied out front, eats all day. Maria's the prettiest. The sheep was out the back till we hung him in strips over the fire. Then there's me, followed by Elena the Smaller. And all the visiting butterflies, snakes and mice. And two brothers; Juan and Pedro. There were two more, but they died. Juan works with Papi all day and Pedro fights with our cousins, hare-lipped José or Diego. He never takes off the leather jacket Uncle Jacinto brought him, full of zips, embroidered with Yanqui flag and eagle – except to sweat in the *temascal*.

Before the stranger arrived nothing much happened. We woke before sun-up, Mami built the fire and smoke filled our hut. Light filtered in through gaps in the slats, while smoke leaked out the corrugated roof. Elena milled coffee. I brought water from the *pila*. Our floor is as bumpy as the mountains about us, everything balanced just so but our bare feet know the curves like we know our own. Mami made eggs and *tortillas*. Maria passed down enamel cups hung on nails and pans slung on a small bush. We handed out bowls from a cupboard and spoons from a bag dangling from the rafters. We sat on stools, the bed or squatted. After breakfast the boys jumped on the bed and threw clothes about. Big girls rolled smaller ones into hammocks of blankets and sang:

> *Vamos a la vuelta, del toro toro gil,*
> *A ver a la rana comiendo perejil.'*

My favourite game, mine alone, was climbing into Uncle Jacinto's shiny grey vinyl suitcase. Maria or Elena the Elder pushed me, bronze wheels bumping over the stones, my eyes peeking above the metal zip, crying at the top of my voice:

'Take me to *la capital.'*

'To the stars.'

or:

'Out of the bowl!'

We got in trouble if we disturbed Papi, snoring in through his flat nose and out through fat lips. He and Juan walk early-early in the night to our land, half-way down the valley and around three bends where we keep three cows and grow maize. They bring home firewood in nets belted around their foreheads. On Sundays they hunt for deer. When Pedro was little he'd look up at each gunshot, wistfully.

The girls stayed home to help cook, scrub clothes, wash dishes and weave *huipils* embroidered with parrots and horses. We hung the corn cobs Papi brought home from the rafters to dry and fill the sacks, bashing them till the kernels came loose. We washed them and boiled them in a cauldron of water and lime, golden nuggets hidden beneath a thick layer of scum. Once cool, we rubbed them till translucent husks fell away and ground them to a clay the colour of sunflowers. At each meal the moon-shaped *comal* was coated with wet lime on the coals. As it heated, continents and oceans shimmered and disappear like those in my dreams and slapping tortillas into shape began.

Buses stopped just below our house. Two left for Nebaj before dawn, horns echoing across the mountains. They returned in late afternoon bringing villagers from the market, chickens bound by the feet, crates of fizzy drinks and foil packets of fried *platinos*. Behind us lay the school, with its slatted windows and barbed fence. The valley spread out below us with its green crescent of lake, like the fragment of mirror we combed our hair in. Cows and sheep grazed in the sloping fields marked with posts and barbed wire. Newer roofs shone silver in the sun, while thatched and rusty roofs were camouflaged amongst banana leaves. Smoke eddied all day from one house or other. Waxy white lilies, yellow *flor de muerto* and violet bells of *jabon* filled the yard.

One day the bus brought the stranger. He was tall and thin with hair like dry corn leaves and skin pink as *carnatira* seeds. He carried a bag with clothes, a box with a glass window, drawings of mountains and an exercise book. On top he'd tied a rolled mat and house of folded sheets. He stayed for a month learning *Ixel* from my sisters. He gave Mami *quetzales* to feed him and talked to Papi about the future.

Papi translated for Mami. In the stranger's country, people had only two or three children. Some had none at all. Papi told him the Church said it was a sin but the stranger didn't seem to think so. What did they do with their land if they didn't have children, asked Papi? The stranger said most didn't, they rented rooms, one on top of the other, like a honeycomb. So where did they grow their vegetables? They got them from shops that bought them from farms. Papi thought about this a while. Then he asked if they were happy. It was the stranger's turn to look confused.

The stranger said there were others like him who wanted to come to Palop. The mountains, he said, were a marvellous treasure and the *Cooperacion* would build a path to connect one village to the next. Papi said there were some already, but the stranger said they needed signs and a certain type of hut, not like ours, all black with smoke, a lumpy floor and mattresses heaped with dirty clothes. They wanted wooden beds, cupboards, a flush toilet and a hot shower. And electricity. Papi scratched his head.

Then, one night, Papi happened to tell him Grandpapi's house had been burnt to the ground by the army. The stranger brightened. He offered to build the hut if Papi would let him use his land (the *Cooperacion* wanted to help mountain folk hit by the Civil War). Visitors would pay and, after Papi paid the *Cooperacion* back, Papi could keep the hut. Papi explained this to Mami, who said nothing, till the stranger had gone. They discussed it for hours and called Uncle Jacinto over to get his opinion.

Made of pale new wood, it stands on red painted cement. It has a shiny roof, a wooden door, two shutters and wires and bulbs for electricity. Inside, a dozen beds with new mattresses, a huge chest and cupboards. Below, a shower room and flush toilet. Three men in green shiny jackets built a trail. Trekkers would come, they promised. For a while we kids weren't allowed to play there but, when no trekkers came, Papi didn't bother shooing us, nor the dogs, out any more. Rainy season cleared into a bright November. Clouds dissolved into storms again. Papi put chickens into the attic, stored bags of feed on the floor and kept his saddle on the chest. When he killed sheep, he hung their skins from the rafters. Mami stored coils of barbed wire under the beds, white plastic chairs, and school books in the cupboards.

The year I became too big to cram myself into the suitcase, new strangers showed up. They carried strap-on bags and leather boots. The women wore trousers. They were upset about chickens in the hut and cold water. More arrived in the weeks that followed. They kept us busy making coffees, *tortillas*, washing sheets and cleaning up.

They stopped coming in rainy season. But when the rains cleared the hut was full again. Each time they left, they gave Mami a wad of money. We were the first in Palop to have electricity. My sisters bought a stereo, my brothers a TV to watch wrestling. Papi bought Mami a gas cooker. Everyone was happy. We had everything we'd ever dreamed of. And many things we hadn't. Elena the Elder got forty thousand *quetzales* together and crossed without papers. Maria married and went to work in a dentist's in Nebaj. Elena the Smaller, the first to finish secondary school, became a teacher in Xalbal. Pedro got a job as a travelling salesman, bringing Tigo mobiles with a hundred and fifty quetzales of credit and a free wind-breaker to Quiché. Papi never understood why they'd left. Only Jacinta the Elder, for whom good fortune came too late, stayed. And Juan who worked the land with Papi.

The winter I stopped going to school, Jacques and his family arrived. He came with a huge grey vinyl suitcase with a silver zip and four bronze wheels that I fit inside. No wonder I fell in love with him. My Spanish was good enough to let him know. His was good enough to give me his word he'd come back. He packed his clothes in a hessian sack and left the suitcase as his guarantee. It took him three years to finish his studies, find work and return.

I put a toothbrush and the *huipil* Mami wove for my wedding day into the suitcase. Papi and Juan gave me hard hugs before they left for the fields. Thumping along that winding, craggy dirt road, hawks circling, I looked back at Mami through the greasy rear window. She kept waving till the fog swallowed her. And I knew I had escaped the bowl for good.

The King and The Light
David Guy

There once was a King who had ruled his kingdom for many years, and there remained no-one who dared to question him. His power was such that there were none upon the earth who he considered his equal, and so one day he called down a star from the night sky and bade her walk with him. It was there, in his vast garden, that he asked her to be his wife.

'Where would I live?' she asked.

'In my castle,' the King replied.

The star laughed, and said she could not, for she was used to the vastness of space, and walls were not to her liking.

'Well then, if not in my castle how about in the fields of my kingdom?' he said, and he showed her the extent of his fields and the vastness of his domain. 'All this is mine, and within it you can go where you please, for you would be Queen and none but I would dare stop you.'

But still she refused.

'Even your kingdom has borders. And borders themselves are walls,' she said. 'Walls of another kind, yes, but they constrain all the same.'

'Then, if not my wife, my prisoner you will be,' the King said, and he called for his guards to capture her.

To this the star replied, 'Wife, servant, prisoner, slave – what difference would it make what you call me? Without choice, the imprisonment is just the same.'

The King's guards led her to the deepest and darkest part of the castle's vast filthy dungeons, and there, in the smallest cell, they locked her inside. 'Perhaps when this cell has dimmed the fire in your heart you will see the error of your ways,' the King said to the star.

To which the star said, 'It is not only me this cell holds in place, for you as well are bound by it.' But the King would not listen, and he left her there, glowing to no-one in the dark.

After a week, the King returned and asked once more for her hand in marriage. The star looked just as bright as before, if not brighter, and still she refused. 'If a week is not enough to change your mind, then so be it,' said the King.

'And to you I say the same,' said the star. But the King would not listen.

After a month, the King returned for a second time, and asked her again to marry him. The star's radiance was brighter than ever and she refused once more. 'If a month is not enough to change your mind, then so be it,' said the King.

'And to you again I say the same,' said the star. But the King would not listen.

After a year, the King returned for a final time. 'I have asked you three times to marry me, and three times you have refused. If you refuse me a fourth time, I shall abandon you here and you shall know nothing more but imprisonment for the rest of your days.'

By now the star was so bright the King had to shield his eyes against her majesty. 'I have spent a year in this cage, hoping each day that you would come to understand that these walls have imprisoned you just as much as me. But you have understood nothing.'

The star reached out and took the King by the hand. 'Look, I shall show you,' she said. And with that her brightness flared and the King's castle was burned to the ground, and the people within were set free.

And then she shone more brilliantly than ever before,

and every wall and building in the country was reduced to ash, although the people within were left unharmed.

And then her brightness exploded outwards once more and the walls and the borders of all the Earth were destroyed and everyone across the world was set free. And in the comfort of her light there was much rejoicing and a shared sense of kinship between all that would never fade.

The people of the world gave her praise, but they did not make a God of her, not even a Queen, for her light had shown them that those that rule are another wall imposed upon the world, and the Gods themselves yet another.

To the King she said, 'To you, and only you, shall I show a truly wall-less world, out beyond the binds of gravity.' And she bore him up into the immensity of space, and took him to the deepest and darkest part of her infinitely vast domain, and she set him down there in the darkness, where the only light was her own, for the rest of the stars were too far away to cast their light upon him.

'Now, my King, you are free.'

And she left him there in the dark, in the cold, far out beyond the walls of the world.

Dog's Life
Alison Lock

New Street precinct is where the shops look out onto a large paved area. On the roadside, there is a row of planters – ashtrays in the daytime, toilets at night. A butcher is standing outside his shop tying his apron-strings behind his back, mop and bucket at his side. He stamps his feet to make the pigeons scatter.

A dog careens around the corner, barely missing the lamppost. It's a perfect mongrel: Labrador build, Spaniel eyes, a Border Collie white patch around one eye. He's cocking a leg by the entrance of the meat shop.

'Hey!' shouts the owner, flicking droplets of disinfectant from the end of his mop.

The dog runs away. The butcher dips his hand into the pocket of his apron, pulls out a mobile phone and presses in a number.

'Always around here. Dirty Devil!' he shouts into the phone. 'Needs shooting, if you ask me.'

I watch the trickle of urine as it snakes along the pavement, wiggling in front of the butcher's feet.

I snigger. He looks up. But before he gets me, I leg it, running down the street and around the corner, straight into the *Hare and Hounds*.

'He's not here. Y'Pa's not here.' The barman says, not even looking up at me as he pulls a pint.

I turn to go but as I reach the door a nuzzling snout appears. It's the dog again, the one from outside the butcher's shop. Nose to the floor, weaving around the bar stools. He gobbles up broken crisps, peanuts brushed from laps. He is varnishing the floor with shiny lick marks. The barman places the pint onto the bar and looks up. Without a word he reaches for a bowl from under the counter and places it on the floor. The dog wags his tail when he sees it, and he skids forward.

'Steady on, Dog!' One of the punters looks down from his perch and smiles. 'Got a thirst on, that one,' says the man, at the same time pushing his glass forward on the bar. 'Pint of Guinness and a drop for our friend here.'

He means the dog. I don't know why but he starts to laugh, his shoulders rising and falling, and he keeps on until his chest crackles and his face flushes the colour of puce. As he gags, another man pats him hard on the back until he coughs up, dislodging the troublesome phlegm.

By now the dog has emptied the bowl and is circling. Around and around he goes. He stops to gnaw his hind quarters, sinking his teeth into a sore-looking hide.

'Fleas,' the man nearest the door says and turns away.

Finally, the dog stops turning, he wobbles and leaves the bar through the swing door. I decide to follow him out onto the street. We are dodging in and out of the crowd in the pink evening light, slowly at first. Then the dog picks up speed, trotting like the Lipizzaners I've seen on the telly, his head held haughty-high. He stops, abruptly, his nose to the ground following the rivulets from a canned drink that is tipped onto its side. Now his nose is buried in a chip wrapper.

A deep voice from behind bellows, 'Oi!'

The dog looks behind him. The dog begins to run. I follow. We bound through a labyrinth of alleyways, leaping over scraps of cars, single doors, mattresses, bags of garden rubbish until we come to a brick wall. Crash! A bin lid has fallen and is rolling in tighter and tighter circles. We turn and together we race along a dirt track at the back of the shops. Ahead, I see a woman seated on a kitchen chair, a curl of smoke rising from her mouth.

'There you are!' she says through lips clasped tightly around a cigarette.

Her hand is held out, the dog's head pushes against her blue housecoat. I hide behind a bin and watch. As she leans forward, loose hairs drift from her white cap. Behind her there are puffs of steam billowing into the evening air, filling it with the scent of hot linen.

'Look at the state of you,' she says. Her voice is a mock caress.

The dog tries to lick her fingers as they reach for his ears, then she pulls at the knots and burrs that are snagged in the fur. 'There,' she says. 'That's better.'

'Who's out there?' A man's muffled voice rumbles through the mist, and a slice of fluorescent light appears through the doorway. 'Who are you talking to, Shell?'

'Never you mind!' the woman calls over her shoulder. She winks at the dog and puts a finger to her lips. 'Wait right here!' she says, tapping the dog's nose. The dog tilts his head. 'I've a special treat for you today!'

Soon the woman in the blue housecoat is back with a serviette wrapped up like a parcel. The dog bolts down the scraps of food and licks her hands clean before she goes back inside.

We're off again, along the canal towpath. He's used to me now, is Dog, running along beside him. He halts to lap at a muddy puddle, but then lurches sideways, head down, and he growls at a sudden movement in the reeds – a rustling. 'It's only a duck,' I say. Dog barks and the swaying leaves are stilled.

We carry on under a bridge where the stench of urine stings my nose, and now we are racing up the stone steps to the road. Dog stands by the kerb, waiting. A truck comes from the right, splashing him head to paw in an oily slick. His coat clings to his bones – he has the ribs of a scavenger.

A gap in the traffic and we are over the other side where there are rows of shops and doorways. Dog is sniffing at old clothes, blankets, bits of torn cardboard.

'Hey you! Come here,' a voice calls from within a doorway.

I hide in the shadows. I see Dog sniffing at the toes that protrude where the leather parts from the soles. He is licking a face, glazing the end of the nose.

'Come on, darling, you stay with me now,' the man says as he slings a piece of string around Dog's neck.

Empty bottles clatter into the gutter, a black van rolls up to the kerbside. The window is wound down.

'That your dog is it?' Two men. One is staring down at Dog, the other is leaning over from the driver's side, peering into the doorway. 'That your dog?' the man repeats.

'Feck you, get away, you...'

'Dosser!' the man calls from the window, and to his mate: 'Come on, let's get out of here.'

The van jolts forward as the gears crunch.

*

'Where've you been out to this late?' Ma demands.

'Nowhere. Just out.'

'Ain't safe this time o' night,' she says. 'What've you been up to?'

'Can I have a dog?' I say. 'I'd look after it.'

'No!' she says. 'For the last time, NO!'

*

Next morning, I'm up early, I take the shortcut through the industrial estate on my way to school. I hear the factory boiler firing up, the clunk of metal on metal. I pass a canteen window just as a hand is latching it open, and the smell of bacon wafts into the morning air. That's when I see Dog, I think of him as *my* dog now. His string leash is dragging behind him. I follow him around the corner to an office block where he defecates onto a neat square of paving. A man in a uniform appears through the swinging doors of silent glass.

'Shoo, you dirty beast!' The dog flinches at the sound of the voice and turns away.

I have to rush to catch up with him now. But there he is, sniffing the ground, pushing his nose into the base of some broken guttering.

Neither I nor the dog see the three men approaching. 'Out of the way, boy,' one says. They come from behind.

'Go on,' I shout to the dog, waving my arms, coaxing him to run off, and just for a moment, he looks up. He sees me, and instead of running, he wags his tail.

'Split up,' one man mouths to the others.

He's the one with a long pole with a loop of rope like a lasso on a stick. The others have their arms outstretched. They are cautious as they move forward, deft-footed.

'Run, Dog, run!' I shout and clap my hands.

The dog lurches to one side, the wrong side. One of the men presses his foot onto the string leash. It tightens around Dog's neck, who bares his teeth, but it is so tight that he cannot even growl. His head is held from behind, as another man lifts him, up, into the back of the van. The doors slam shut.

I run up to the van shouting, bang it with my fist, but I am choked by the fumes from the revving engine. I hear Dog's claws scratching the metal floor as the van jolts forward. I run and run, following the van, swooping around corners, on and on until it is out of sight, heading towards the north end of town.

'Seven days in a cage,' explains Dale. 'They're fed, watered, taken for a trot around the compound and then, well...' He looks doubtful. 'The lucky ones get claimed, the rest are put down.' Dale knows all about it. His mum works at the place where they take them. It's on Grant Street next to the Council Buildings.

I can't stop thinking about Dog: whimpering in a cage, the kennel staff trying their best, but they know he's a street dog, an old mongrel, and nobody will want him.

Saturday morning, and I'm delivering newspapers. At the *Hare and Hounds*, the landlord is up and about. The morning sun shines through the window and I read the reflection of the word SNUG on the back wall – it says GUNS. I chuck a paper into the entrance porch. It slaps onto the tiled floor.

Traffic rumbles at a steady pace on the road bridge over the canal. Some people are unlocking metal doors or pulling down canopies with long hooked poles. He's not there now – the man who slept with the dog.

I deliver the papers to the terraces of houses along Marple Street and Victoria Road, then I take the short cut through Broad Bank and on to New Street. The cafe has its chairs and tables set out on the pavement. A shower of rain has varnished the surfaces, and they dazzle in the sunlight. There's no-one else about to see the old man shuffling along.

'Where's my dog?' he croaks when he sees me.

There's a trickle of soapy water darting between the slabs of the pavement as the butcher appears. A van goes by – a black van with grilled windows. The driver sees the butcher and gives him the thumbs up. The butcher whistles a tune as he lays out his goods on the table by the entrance – ready-cooked chickens, packets of pork chops, fat sausages, rib-eye steaks – all in neat rows. He stands back with his hands on his hips.

'Got a bone for an old dog?' the old man asks.

The butcher turns. He shakes his head, spits onto the ground, and goes back inside the shop. The cellophane on the meat reflects the morning sun.

The old man walks on, stumbling around the lampposts,

a cooked chicken under his arm.

I'm on the road where the launderette gushes out its fresh steam. I have an idea, and I nip around the back. Inside, the machines sound like rockets about to take off and the floor shivers with the power of the spin cycle. I can see the corner of her blue coat through the open door. Shell is sitting on a high stool, dipping a biscuit into her coffee. She is surprised to see me but she listens when I tell her about Dog. As soon as I've finished, she pulls her jacket around her shoulders and shoves her handbag under one arm.

'Back in a jiffy,' she calls out over her shoulder, and she takes my arm and winks.

'Where you off to?' It's the voice of the man from the mist.

But we're already heading down the lane to the bus stop on the main road.

'One and a half to Grant Street,' she says to the driver, pulling the coins from her purse.

She looks at me and smiles. 'We are on a mission,' she says. 'A mission to free Dog.'

Si nos disseisivimus vel elongavimus Walenses de terris vel libertatibus vel rebus aliis, sine legali judicio parium suorum, in Anglia vel in Wallia, eis statim reddantur; et si contencio super hoc orta fuerit, tunc inde fiat in Marchia per judicium parium suorum: de tenementis Anglie secundum legem Anglie; de tenementis Wallie secundum legem Wallie; de tenementis Marchie secundum legem Marchie. Idem facient Walenses nobis et nostris.

If we have deprived or dispossessed any Welshmen of land, liberties, or anything else in England or in Wales, without the lawful judgment of their equals, these are at once to be returned to them. A dispute on this point shall be determined in the Marches by the judgment of equals. English law shall apply to holdings of land in England, Welsh law to those in Wales, and the law of the Marches to those in the Marches. The Welsh shall treat us and ours in the same way.

Border Country
David Mathews

We were badly in need of diversion, Buck, Rhys and me.

Events had stirred us. After the embarrassment of the theft of the World Cup, when Pickles the mongrel found it – his the only English paws likely come near it, we reckoned – we found it uplifting that it was wrapped in newspaper, like chips. When Labour won the election we felt the modern world had arrived, the toffs being put in their place. But these were passing joys, and though the days had lengthened, Easter had come without redemption for us, only limitless revision for looming A-Levels, those tests of intellect, rigour and competence that, we were told, would shape our lives.

Bank holiday Monday. Buck and I had absconded from our respective cells to Rhys's for consoling cake, Rhys's mum boosting our morale if not our IQs by kidding us that lemon sponge was good for the Welsh brain. Then, 'Take a day off,' she said. 'Go somewhere. Stop feeling sorry for yourselves, and give us a break.'

'Why not?' said Buck. 'There's no cricket, but we could go abroad, so to speak, to England and see the lions.'

Rhys and I assumed he had in mind London Zoo or Bristol, but he was thinking of the new safari park. The lions, though wandering free, had not eaten anyone important enough to make the papers, so there was a chance they had not yet acquired a taste for human flesh.

'What do you suppose lions make of Somerset?' We

decided that the delights of cider, real cheddar cheese from Cheddar and the sands of Weston-super-Mare would be lost on lions, which might leave them disinclined to be watched. Anyway, how must they feel, being peered at by the public as they ate, crapped or set about the continuance of the species?

Not the lions then.

'What about Offa's Dyke? We could jump from Wales into England and back again, or cross through secret glades like cockle and laverbread smugglers from the Gower.' This was Buck, building up a head of romantic steam, as per.

A border town would be good, I suggested. We made too little of them now that Welsh pubs opened on the Sabbath. My grandfather had come from Leominster, with its ducking stool for scolds.

We counted up the women, starting with our sisters, who would qualify as scolds. We decided quite a few men were eligible too, but, 'We'll have no more of that, Lewis', said Rhys's mother, overhearing my contribution to a longish list. 'Mrs Cadwallader's not all bad you know.'

Rhys thought Ludlow, on account of his studying Housman's poetry. He gave us the bit about blue remembered hills. 'It's the place to go. He mentions it more than any other town or village. He never lived there, mind, he wasn't even from Shropshire.'

Mr Evans at the station told us over the phone that British Rail would take us to Ludlow, provided we asked nicely. An AA guide book told us of the town's delights, including a castle, a commanding position over two rivers and decent pubs. Rhys read us more Housman, about Ludlow lads, their loves and their deaths, especially their deaths – enough sorrow and loss to get Buck's vote.

We found we had enough for the train fare and a pint or two, but even with a picnic lunch, we would have to swear off the temptations of Dewi's café – principally Dolores – and the fleshpots of Barry Island for a while. No bad thing for less than ardent revisers, according to Buck's logic. 'How can anyone revise really hard *without* going to Ludlow?'

Rhys's mother agreed and sent Buck and me back to our equations and thermodynamics.

On Friday, Mr Evans having consented to sell us excursion tickets, we made our perilous way into border country.

In Ludlow everything that mattered was up the hill, high above the station. Even without the castle it would have been a town to boss the surrounding country. Not a place you would mess with if you were inclined to insurrection. Mind you, some of the people thereabouts had been smart, Rhys had learned. Border regions attracted a shrewder rogue, able to exploit confusion over who had the right to detain you, judge you or slay you for looking foreign.

We found de Grey's, a posh café that had been in Ludlow since the middle ages. Nothing like Dewi's; the proprietor seemed pleased to see us. The waitress was about 110 years old, only in her bright efficiency comparing with Dolores. She gave us a rundown on the town, sent us off to see where Housman's ashes were, and suggested we might like the livestock market. Why she thought we might be interested in sheep or cattle, goodness knows. Maybe that's what stirred lads in those parts, that and haymaking with its attendant diversions.

Housman's ashes were marked by a plaque with his full name. 'You don't think of him as an Alf, not with him being a prof,' Buck said. 'Perhaps that's why he used initials, to discourage intimacy.'

'Let's go and see the cattle now. Perhaps there'll be a prize bull.'

'Perhaps it'll escape and rampage about, like in Spain, or like the lions in the safari park.'

'They'll have to fire tranquilliser darts to bring it down,

but they'll miss and hit some local beauty instead, and she'll sleep in the castle tower for 100 years until she's woken by a kiss from a spaceman, back from Mars.'

From a distance the massed livestock seemed to sport flat caps and trilbies, and we took the mist above them to be their breath condensing in the cool air. But the headgear wearers turned out to be scores of farmers eyeing sheep and cattle, and the cloud around them came from the Capstans in the corners of their mouths.

What pleased us was that there was a row in progress, shouting, waving arms and threats. No fists though. The action centred on a round enclosure with a raised platform on its perimeter where an auctioneer stood. The place had the air of a bear pit.

Hearing us puzzle over what was going on, a cub reporter for the local paper put us in the picture.

'That cow in the ring, she's a Hereford been brought for sale by that plum-faced chap there, Griff Jones, farms over the border. Miserable bugger. You don't want to meet him after he's had too much. And those two women, it's their cow that Jones was grazing and milking for them. But he says, as they're from England and he's in Wales, he's got the right to sell the cow. And before you ask, there's no paperwork and the police don't want to know. And I hope they hurry up, because I have to file the story.' At that he lit a ciggie, pulled his hat aslant, and pretended he was digging into vice in the Chicago stockyards.

The cow's name was Daisy. 'Had to be,' said Buck.

Rhys seemed agitated. 'He can't do that, Mr Jones can't, not after 1215.'

I pointed out that it was only 1145. Rhys looked at me with scorn, having meant the year 1215 and Magna Carta. Next moment he was gone, talking to Daisy's owners, and before Buck and I could work out what he was about, Rhys was button-holing the auctioneer, two handsome women in tow.

Rhys had mentioned Magna Carta once, at Dewi's café, Dewi himself in attendance, stopwatch in hand, monitoring our rate of purchase. Rhys habitually shared with Buck and me whatever he had been reading before he left the house. Had we read it, Magna Carta?

Neither of us had, to be honest. The nearest we had come to it was *1066 and All That*, which described it as the cause of democracy in England, except for the common people. Rhys, shocked, offered to enlighten us. We stood to leave.

'No, wait,' he said. 'It says something about Wales. Wales specifically.'

He described the post-Norman Conquest relationship between Wales and England as tetchy on a good day and downright rapacious most of the time. In their negotiations with the king, the barons had wangled equality for Welsh law. Rhys quoted a phrase or two, about Welshmen having returned to them anything that had been appropriated, 'without the lawful judgment of their equals'. And another bit, probably the reason Wales was mentioned at all, 'The Welsh shall treat us and ours in the same way'.

The Ludlow auctioneer was a tall man, imposing, as you might need to be. Before you could say 'King John was a Bad King', he had restored order with the liberal use of his gavel. 'Auctioneers talk really fast,' said Buck, 'in a drone with twiddly bits. Do you suppose they talk like that at home, and have masses of kids because they never give their wives a chance to say no?'

But this auctioneer spoke at human speed. 'Now then, about this cow… Daisy.' As he said the cow's name, he looked pained. Buck reckoned that in the business of selling beasts for breeding or the table, names did not come into it much. 'This young man,' here he indicated Rhys, 'believes he has a solution to our dilemma. Simmer down… and you Mr Jones. Three points. One. As you gentlemen know, Ludlow was, is, and always will be the principal town of the Marches.' There was a rumble of agreement. 'Point two. It seems from ancient treaty that disputes when Welshmen or Englishmen – or English women – have been, what was it… ?' he consulted Rhys, and, smiling broadly, continued, '…have been deprived or dispossessed of something without the lawful judgment of their equals, whether in England or Wales, we have to give it them back. Point three. In the case of dispute, it's the law of the Marches that decides it. Clear?'

His audience was not clear. Hands went up with half formed questions and went down again; but Rhys looked triumphant. Buck and I had never seen him put his book knowledge to such dramatic use. The auctioneer – James Farrier, the newsman told us – proposed that in matters concerning the law of the Marches, in his livestock market he had delegated powers. He was enjoying himself. 'Anyone disagree with that?' No-one did, not even Griff Jones, leaning on the barrier of the sale ring like a man who had gone a round with Henry Cooper.

'Right then. You now decide, as the Miss Bennetts' equals, whether I sell said cow Daisy to the benefit of Mr Jones here, or reinstate her to the Miss Bennetts?' The crowd cottoned on, and the place was filled with shouts of 'Bennett', 'Sell' and, 'I'll take the two lasses.'

Mr Farrier called for a show of hands, and the proposal to sell was thrown out by several millions to one. Cheering followed, with much backslapping, hugs and kisses in the vicinity of Rhys and Mr Farrier. A local man offered to keep Daisy with his herd, saying also that if the Misses Bennett wanted calves, he could put Daisy to the bull.

We never ate our picnic, not till the train home anyway. We were taken for a slap-up lunch by Sarah and Alison Bennett.

Buck fell in love, as per. Mr Farrier joined us for pudding, still aglow with the fun of it, and bought us pints.

A daft day, we agreed on the train, but satisfying, thanks to Rhys and the long-ago barons. No revision, a handsome town, a rare carry-on with justice done, a meal with two nice women, our beer bought for us and change in our pockets. Rhys searched his Housman for something that fitted the day, but since no-one had died or marched away to fight for Queen and Empire, we made do with our own nattering, and speculation as to what life might bring.

Knitting for Demons
Cherry Potts

The phone is ringing. It woke me up, I realise, as the sense of urgency translates into *bring-bring–bring-bring*. It is an old fashioned phone, the colour of overcooked string beans, with a dial, and a curly cord. It keeps ringing; there is no voicemail to take a message.

I can feel the thrum of its insistence before I quite touch the receiver. It makes an indignant ping as I pick it up.

'Hello?' I ask nervously. Who would ring me here?

Hello, a voice says, crackling with echo, like long distance calls used to, redolent with the ghost of other conversations, trapped in cables under oceans the world round.

So how are things going? the voice asks.

'Going?' I say, trying to recognise the voice. Female, older than me…?

Yes, she says. *How far have you got to?*

I look round blankly. *Got to?* Was I meant to be getting somewhere? Now I think about it, this is a bit like a station waiting room, grey-walled, featureless, apart from a small two-bar electric fire, circa 1965, in the corner. A table, and a few upright chairs bolted to the floor.

'I'm waiting.' I say, absentmindedly knitting my fingers into the cord.

For what? she asks. That gets me. *Permission*, I think, but I don't say it.

Whose permission? she asks.

'How did you…?'

…know what you were thinking? I'm just clever that way. Permission for what, anyway?

Now I'm stumped. I don't know what I'm doing here, and I don't know where it was I was meant to be going, it can't have been important, nothing I do is important.

Who's that talking? she asks, and I look round. She's right; there was someone else there for a moment.

'I don't know,' I say. Why would I know?

Hold up, she says, *there it is again. Where's it coming from?*

I look round again.

What does it look like, that voice?

Even through the crackles and the deep-sea echo, there's a change to her voice, crisper, not to be argued with.

I know where it is; it's just behind me, in my blind spot. If I were to turn quickly, I'd catch it. But I don't want to turn, don't want to look…

If you did look, what would you see? she asks patiently.

'Nothing.' I say.

What kind of nothing?

A big nothing which can eat me alive with the acid of its contempt.

That's some kind of nothing, she says, *kind of scary.*

She's doing it again, mind reading.

'Yes,' I say. 'Yes, I'm scared of it.'

What can it do to you? she asks.

What can't it do? It can destroy me, drop by drop with scorn and derision.

Are you listening? she says.

'To what?' I ask, hardly able to hear her over the hornet drone of hate in my other ear.

She sighs. Of course she does, she's wasting her time with me, there's nothing she can do to untangle my snare.

Swat that wasp. A folded newspaper appears at my elbow.

'It's too big,' I whisper.

How big is too big? she asks, as the newspaper grows and grows until it is too heavy to lift. *How about making it smaller instead? What would it be like if it was a teensy weenie gnat?*

The hornet-voice recedes to a whine: high-pitched, evil, dangerous; mosquito deadly. I flinch as it dives to spit vitriol into my ear.

Hmm, she says. *If this voice were a person who would it be?*

'My father,' I say without thinking, and there he is, behind my left shoulder, his shadow flung across the table, hand reaching to cut me off.

'No!' I say, cradling the phone against me and getting the table between us. It isn't much of a barrier, and I have to look at him now. He doesn't look much like himself, stronger, and taller, and …not really my father at all.

'You aren't my father,' I say, noticing something of a feminine aspect, now that I look carefully.

A tinny voice squeaks at me and I put the receiver back to my ear.

'What?' I say.

When are you going to go?

'What?' I ask again, glancing beyond him to the door. 'I can't leave.' What a ridiculous idea.

What stops you?

'I don't know what's out there.'

The door is open, I hadn't noticed that before. There is light out there, but it feels like a stage set – as though there's nothing substantial out there, perhaps not even a floor.

Go and see, she says. I stay rooted to the spot. The hornet-father sneers at me. *Coward,* it mouths. I look at the doorway, and my knees fail me, I sit down hard.

'I can't.'

You don't have to, she says gently.

You can decide for yourself what's there. What would you like to be out there?

'Trees,' I say immediately. 'A river.'

Big trees? she asks.

'No, young birches – tall and willowy.'

Some willows too then, for the river?

'Yes,' I say, smiling in spite of myself.

What's the river like?

'Broad and slow,' I say, 'dappled in sunlight, buzzing with drowsy summer bees, dusty with fallen pollen.'

Sounds nice, she says.

'It is,' I say, remembering the meadow running down to the water and the fringing of trees shading the cows standing knee deep in the slow water.

What's that wonderful smell? she says. *Is it honeysuckle?*

'No, I don't think so, I don't know its name, but it's pretty.'

What else? she asks.

A heron, stock-still on the bank, and a kingfisher on the branch of that tree there, and buzzards circling lazy thermals above.

What is it about birds?

'Freedom.' I say, and I'm back in the waiting room.

So, what's through the door? she asks.

I smile.

Yes? she asks.

'Yes,' I agree.

So, we know what's out there now, she says. *You can smell the flowers, you can hear the water and the buzzards, yes? You can feel the summer breeze.*

'Yes,' I say eagerly, taking a step towards the door.

It's not safe; you'll never been able to cope on your own, who'll look after you?

He's there again, barring the way. My heart pounds: frustration, disappointment; failure.

The light beyond the door fades.

Whoa, she says, *what's happening?*

'I… I can't do it.'

What do you need so that you can?

I can't answer, I don't know what it's like to be the kind of strong I need to be.

Ok, she says. *Who do you know who is strong?* I look at the dark figure in front of me.

If you must, she says. *How does he do it?*

How does he do it?

'He doesn't,' I say at last. 'I let him. It's mostly bluff.'

So bluff, she says. *What will let you be strong?*

'He has to be weak.'

How's that going to work?

I can't imagine him weak.

There is an odd clicking noise coming from somewhere, like mandibles on a cockroach. I can't bear to look at him.

What about a cockroach is weak? she asks.

I imagine stepping on him, but no, that feels terrible.

'I can't fight him.'

You don't need to. What would make him less scary?

I realise now that the clicking is coming down the phone. I listen, trying to identify the noise.

'Are you… knitting?'

Yes, she says.

'What are you knitting?'

Well, there's a pause and I imagine her turning the needles for a new row; *right now, I'm knitting a Fair Isle jumper for your insect demon. What colours would you like?*

The curly cable from the receiver uncoils and whips across the room and starts to ravel up around him. He raises his arms in alarm.

'Yellow, and red – purple – how many colours have you got?'

As many as you need, she says.

It's not a very good jumper; the sleeves are far too long, trailing to the ground.

'Day-Glo pink,' I say, as she reaches the neck.

How's that? she asks.

'Awesome,' I say, grinning. He looks horrified and embarrassed, and young suddenly, maybe six years old.

He glares at me. A six year old who pulls the wings off flies.

This won't do you any good in the long run, he says.

'Says who?' I say, and the Fair Isle ravels further, knitting itself up over his mouth, his nose, his eyes… it finishes with a neat turquoise bobble-hat pompom. There is an indignant but muffled curse.

I laugh.

Ah, she says, *what's that I hear?*

I don't answer her, watching him blunder about snagging his feet on the length of the sleeves, trammelled and half blinded by his woollen all-in-one.

'Hang on,' I say, and put the phone down on the table, the receiver carefully beside it.

I guide him to a chair, settle him down, and pour a cup of tea. The cup is the same dull grey-green as the telephone. I don't know how he will drink it, but I expect he'll work it out.

I pat him on the shoulder and turn back to the phone, but it has gone. In its place is a pink mobile. I pick it up. The display shows a photograph of my river, my heron just taking flight.

I put it to my ear.

'Are you still there?' we say together.

'Just leaving,' I say.

The sun streams through the early summer leaves, the grass is fresh and cool underfoot, still damp and pliant. The scent of cow parsley washes over me. High up a buzzard mews.

Right ho, she says. *You know where to find me.*

'Yes,' I say, as I close the mobile and slip it into my pocket. 'I certainly do.'

Liberty
Andrew McCallum

I was born to know you and to name you
I write you in the sand and snow
on every page I read
on the white sheets of lovemaking
on the crowns of kings and their weapons of mass
destruction
I write you on the echoes of my childhood
on nests and bushes
on wondrous nights of starlight
on the moon swimming in the loch
on the wings of birds
on the beating pulse of windmills
I write you on the first drawn breath of dawn
on the white foam of the clouds and the grey insipid rain
I write you on every wakening path
on every opening gate
I write you among the scattered rocks on demented
mountains
I write you on the threshold of my door
in the fire's sacred stream
on the lamp when it gives light
on the lamp when it is doused
I write you on my bed's empty shell
on my mirror and my reflected room
I write you on my dog
on her listening ears and her clumsy paws
I write you on the ravaged refugees

on all the dispossessed
on their fallen walls and naked solitude
on all that has become absent for them
I write you on health regained
on danger past
on memory and hope
I was born to know you and to name you

Wigtown Bay, 1685
Elinor Brooks

Two women are tied to posts
at the mouth of the Blednoch stream
'to stand till the flood overflows them,
and they drown'.

By the time the sea water swells
the channels of Blednoch and Cree,
runs through the cracks
in saltmarsh blocks,
covers the purslane and samphire,
the arrow-grass, scurvy-grass, aster -
the women's mouths and lungs
will be full, and the psalms
the young one was singing
stoppered.

The blizzard of Arctic birds that
wintered on the merse are moving on:
a few Greylags pluck the grass,
the white-cheeked Barnacles
have gone, and the last lines of Pink-foot
drift across the sky, heading for Greenland.
Craters of shell cling
under the drift-wood, seaweed
streaming downwards from open mouths,
life hanging.

At sunrise, the hunter lowers his gun
as two geese break through the water's sheen:
underwings gleaming,
they wheel into the sun.

The Fool's Tale
Katy Darby

A wise man once said, 'Some are born foolish, some achieve foolishness, and others have foolishness thrust upon them,' – or something like that, anyway. He was no fool, but I am, as you can probably tell. It's not the rustle of bells gives it away, for a man can step out of one costume and into another quick as a chuckle can turn to a frown; nor is it my madcap colours, quartered like a coat of arms, but there's something about a good fool: folk just know.

The natural, or simple fool is born foolish, and there's nothing God nor man can do about it. Mayhap his wits are porridge-thick, his eyes avoid each other, or his face wears a permanent blank grin like a dog's – might even be all three. He could live out his days as the indulged idiot of a superstitious village, the scorned butt of a whole court's jokes, or, more usually, not at all. Them as can't fend for themselves must have someone to defend them, and it's a fortunate fool whose mother lives long enough and earns bread enough to keep her and him both above ground. The simple fool's fate – in fact, the fate of all fools – is either comedy or tragedy. There's nothing in between.

The lucky fool has foolishness thrust upon him, as well as many other things – in the fairytales, he's the one who does everything wrong but still ends up with the princess and half the kingdom, and the king near enough begging him to take the other half. This serendipitous fellow is an honest idiot – not backward, exactly, but not the tallest ear in the wheatfield either. His transparent simplicity is his saving grace – he's not sharp enough to lie, cheat or steal without getting caught, so he's just wise enough not to try. The lucky fool always falls on his feet; I warrant there's a few reading now, wondering but not questioning how they got this house, this wench, that job.

Riddle me this, masters: when is a fool not a fool?

Give up? Never, that's the answer. A fool is a fool always and forever. That's the worst thing about it. The ploughman gets to stow his ploughshare after sunset and on the Sabbath; a priest cannot be always preaching and praying; but a fool must be foolish all the time – no lord wants a jester who is half the time burbling nonsense and the rest of it fox-clever. Dangerous, that'd be. Don't believe all you've heard about the wise-foolish clowns who speak truth to power and advise their lieges on matters of state on the sly: that's the last thing any king's pride could accommodate, and kings have a fearful deal of pride – trust me, I've known a few.

The observant among you may have noticed that I have missed off my list the third and last kind of fool, he who achieves foolishness. This cunning fellow crafts his cretinism, swots up on stupidity and buffs his buffoonery until it shines. This clever fool hides his light under a bushel, for that light could burn him else. This kind of fool is born too wise, too quick, with eyes that see far too much, and soon realises that nobody likes a smart boy so sharp he could cut himself – or someone else. That such boys, unless they're packed away to a monastery to learn their letters and debate with the ancients and the saints, don't often live to be men, one way or another. A fool, on the other hand, is harmless; that is the point of him, nobody fears a fool, for there is no-one slower or lower.

Very well, says this too-bright young man to himself, *here's safety – I shall be the silliest fool that ever England saw! I shall riddle and rhyme, babble and giggle, caper and cower and shake my bells like a milking cow, and nobody will ever envy or hate me, and I shall get three meals a day and all the ale I can sup, for a drunken fool is still funnier.*

You have guessed it, I can see; you are no fool, or if you were you are becoming wise. I am that young man. I am that clever fool. I was not born imbecilic, but I flatter myself I can gurn, drool, and trip over my own tangled, turned-up toes with the dimmest dunce that ever drew breath.

Why then, am I telling you this? Because my disguise is too perfect and complete; I have no-one to confide in, not a single soul, and besides, if you told anyone at court that Runcie had an ounce of wit in his big potato head, they'd laugh you out of the gate. I have counterfeited idiocy for too long: I sometimes fear that the mask has become the face, or rather the jingling cap the cranium, and I have to creep into the broken tower and solve equations and write Latin acrostics until the urge to unveil myself passes. That is the way a good fool become a dead fool in very short order: you don't answer back, and you never, never say anything sensible, even by accident.

I say, I say, I say: when does a clown wear a crown?
Answer: when he's the King of Frankland!

(Or Ruritania, or Nordgard, or whomever we are at war with at the time). My lord Berhain does love that one: rhymes, puns and insulting riddles are about his level. His brother Edric has a taste for filthy jokes, of which I have a vast stock that I tell as if I do not understand them. He calls me to his chamber sometimes, very late, and has me tell them to whatever maid he's swiving that night, and slaps his meaty thighs and roars when some of the younger girls don't understand them either. With a cocked eyebrow and a meaning glance, he offers to enlighten them there and then, while I look on and grin foolishly, my mouth hanging a little open like a happy hound's. Sometimes the kitchen wenches and laundresses and backstairs Betties look at me with more interest than they do Edric, for there is a persistent myth that he whom God has under-endowed in the organ of the brain is often handsomely compensated elsewhere. This is a myth I do not see any reason to dispel, and I have taken advantage of servant-girls' curiosity once or twice – without, of course, revealing my true nature to them. They seem to enjoy my simple, brutish enthusiasm for rutting, and more than that, my silence – for it's a fool indeed who talks nonsense when he's not being paid to, and thus when I am not in the presence of my lord, my lady or his brother, my lips are sealed tight as an abbess's thighs. That's a phrase my lord Edric taught me.

And so I pratfall down the smooth-worn stone steps of the throne room, trip into the tapestries and croon my nincompoop nursery songs to the five-year-old heir, Tyvon (who is the only person in court who can truly appreciate them on my level) – and I am content. I believe myself to be alone in this among King Berhain's immediate circle; Queen Angess loathes her crass husband, Lord Edric envies and plots against him, and everyone else soils themselves in fear of him. We have all learned to tremble at his deadly, sudden rages, his baseless accusations of treachery – levelled, as far as I can tell, at random victims only to keep the rest of his subjects on their toes – and his cruel delight in violent bloodsports. Many wish King Cyned alive again – but under their breath, and not for long, if Berhain catches wind of it.

'Cyned was clever, but weak,' my lord is fond of saying. 'Always had his head in a book – so one day I made sure he left it there!'

Queen Angess has learned to laugh at this feeble joke, even though it is at the expense of her murdered husband. The listener who does not split his sides at King Berhain's sallies 'will have them split for him': another of my lord's witticisms.

Knock knock.
Who's there?

'Runcie, my lady. You said you were melancholy tonight; I am come to cheer you.'

There is a short stillness and silence, and then her heavy oak door creaks open and the Queen stands there, alone, in a simple burgundy gown bereft of jewels and gold-lace, her hair uncoiffed.

My surprise must show on my face, for she says 'I have dismissed Serma for the evening; come in.'

Good. Serma is smooth-faced and hard-eyed and has no sense of humour whatever.

'My Queen,' I say, and enter, tripping over the wolfskin on the floor and catching myself just in time on one twisted post of the bed. But even this supreme piece of physical comedy fails to raise a smile from my mistress. The Queen's lovely, pale face is worn and she gestures me wearily to a settle beside which is a decanter of Rhenish wine and two goblets.

'Pour deep ones,' she says, and sighs. There are some who resent my lady Angess; for her wit, for her beauty, for her power, but mostly because she was not born noble, but achieved it through those first two attributes. When King Cyned married a serving wench they said he was mad, and weak, and all of the things Berhain loves to list, but the fact remains that Berhain still had to wed the widow to cement his claim to the murdered King's throne, and that's because most of the people love and respect her. When Berhain slaughtered her only son, Cyned's heir, the good folk wept for her; she only saved her daughters by agreeing to marry the man. Many hoped that their cursed union would be barren; but then Tyvon was born. The people were cast down, but my lady breathed a sigh of relief. Not to have produced a male heir would have made her position very precarious indeed. Only I know what she went through to have the little lad, for we are friends from a long time ago, when she was plain Angess and I was that strange freak of nature, a stable boy who could read, and taught the kitchenmaid how.

'Edric's been plotting,' she says shortly.

I lift my goblet in resignation. 'Nothing changes.'

She turns and stares at me. 'This time he has had help. Someone with sense and determination. Heaven knows who.'

I think about determined women: backstairs Betties and lusty laundresses. I wonder where Serma is spending her sudden night off. 'How far has it got?' I ask.

She grimaces. 'Poison has been acquired, I hear. You could find out more. Will you? For me?'

'The banquet's tomorrow,' I say. 'That's when I'd do it. Wouldn't you?'

A half-sad smile. 'If I could. But Tyvon...'

'I understand,' I say, and drain my goblet, for courage. The Queen has not touched hers. 'I'll know by tomorrow. I'll come soon as I can.'

What's the only thing worse than being ruled by King Berhain? Being ruled by King Edric.

If Edric murders his brother and seizes the throne, little Tyvon will be the next to go – if, before that, the kingdom doesn't descend into anarchy, chaos and civil war. So her hated husband must be kept alive. If only they could both be got rid of, the whole land would breathe a sigh of relief – but how could that happen? And moreover, who then, would rule?

Never underestimate a serving-maid. After I report back

in detail on Edric and Serma's rather crude conspiracy, I am more than a little surprised that King Berhain falls facedown and foaming into his plateful of lamprey a mere three hours later, at the height of the banquet. Only when Edric is accused of the murder and undeniable evidence produced to prove him guilty do I understand. The Queen, in her role as Regent, presides over the public trial and sentences him to death: the look on her face as the axe falls is that of Edric when I had told him an especially filthy joke.

The mutter now – after the initial shock, outcry, and finally relief when it became clear that my lady was more than capable of ruling in her son's stead until he comes of age – is one of fear that the boy might turn out like his dreadful father. What if, when he reaches his majority, the cycle of bloodshed, civil strife and mad, unwinnable wars should come again? It is a reasonable concern: only a fool would not share it.

And I am that fool. For if Tyvon takes after his father, all that means is that he will be strangely attractive to servant-girls, surprisingly well-endowed, and far too clever to let anyone know how clever he is. Not such a bad fate after all, I'd say – for him or for the country.

When does a clown wear a crown?
Perhaps you'll see, in a dozen years or so. In the meantime, how should I know? I'm only the fool.

Tabernacle Lane
Jeremy Dixon

a line of men waiting
found tiny in the classifieds
the Bouncer smiles
let the music decide

to dare to dance with Divine
be sure of every cheap reaction
take pride in his hand step on stage
a couple of shoulders to trespass on

here's what my mother never did tell me
how that velvet staircase awaits
lit by the pulse of treacherous fairy lights
leads to what can't be seen in the dark

wipe armpit sweat with a Kleenex
to hurl at the howling crowd
never apologise never hide
never let hate be unopposed

O is the story of Bobby O
GQ man desperate for a pen
desperate for a telephone number
his bloom of future possibilities

thrown from scorched roofs
strung on barbed wire
blitzed in the dance of Saturday night
for love and lov an luv & ♥

Flax, San Francisco
Jeremy Dixon

He spends his first
night on Market Street
excited in a paper store,
browsing Japanese
hand-mades and
discontinued Letraset,
watching leather men
choose portfolios.
He stays until closing,
treks to bar six in
Time Out's top-ten,
swinging a Letterpress bag.

Pearls Over Shanghai
Jeremy Dixon

he spends his last night
in the Castro
at a Cockettes revue

the man beside
says he knew Sylvester
says he knew Thom Gunn

and he is impressed
impressed by a septuagenarian
drag queen thumping keys

impressed by crotchless
harem pants
impressed

by a heart-trimmed
dominatrix
whipping straights

he's asked back to see a film
but it's far too late already
for flying tomorrow

he walks back
past auto shops
Mondrian feeling strong

Character Study
Katy Darby

He gets there early by over an hour, and has to buy a tart, biscuit-brown mug of tea in the café opposite to pass the time. He picks over a battered copy of the *Sun*, checking out the other customers, wondering if they're visitors, like him. No: not like him. Friends and family. Husbands and children, maybe. A lot of them have a poor look about them, a betting-shop, Mayfair-smoking look: he scolds himself for noticing and judging, conflating class and criminality. But statistically (he defends himself) poverty and poor education *are* factors in crime, just as crime is a symptom of poverty and poor education.

Better not mention that when he gets inside, though.

He gulps his tea, which has gone from scalding to tepid while he's been staring blankly at what Christine from Dagenham's breasts have to say about the Euro, and checks his watch. The email had said to get there early; that there might be searches. He's worn his newest boxers, imagining airport security; his knackered messenger-bag sorted through carefully by a latex-gloved, unsmiling uniform; the impassive itemisation of the random objects that lurk in its depths; combs, chewing gum, lighters, biros (lots of biros, leaking darkly into the furry suede bottom) notebooks, gas-bills, USB sticks, dongles, widgets, whatsits, Wotsits, cycle-clips, paperclips, pips and grit and other bits.

He realises he's composing a little poem in his head already. Maybe this workshop will come in handy after all. He's not written a word for six months and even a poem would be better than nothing. The last book didn't sell too well, got so-so reviews in the papers and, worse, on Amazon, and the advance for this one ran out last year. That's why he's back on the teaching circuit: that's why, when the University post didn't come through, he said he'd do the prison job instead.

Maybe he'll find it fulfilling, helping old lags find their inner children and stimulate their souls and do something, anything, to pass the time, lodged in their lives like a kidney stone that can't be cut out. (Unsure about that last simile, he mentally scores a line through it). Then again, probably not. Still, fear can be inspirational. New experiences can kickstart new ideas. He's gone through the routine, the writing exercises, so many times that they no longer do anything for him, but sometimes the students seem to find them useful, or fun at least. He checks his watch, heaves up his bag, and starts towards the spiked, towering gates.

He wonders what they'll be like. He wonders if any of them will be able to write. He gives a twisted snort. At least one of them will probably turn out to be better than him.

*

He can't remember the last time he was alone in an all-female group: even at the Institute there's usually another token bloke or two. He doesn't spend much time surrounded by the opposite sex (more's the pity), and gets uneasy when he feels outnumbered, especially in class. There's something weird and archaic about imparting his perceived wisdom to a group of women eager to please; at once pleasurable and shameful. Shame his editor would never go for a romance set in prison;

it could be a whole new subgenre. Goodbye Burberry, *bonjour* Broadmoor. *Au revoir*, heaving bosoms, hello Holloway. He smirks, then bites his lip. They're all looking at him. He doesn't like being looked at at the best of times, but this is something else. He's pretty sure the organisers – and the prisoners – had assumed Frankie Roseward was female, but it's too late now.

There's a strong sour smell of sweat and rolling tobacco in the dingy Activities Room, and an almost palpable air of fuck-or-fight coming off some of the pris – *students*, they're just students. It's genuinely unsettling. Some look eager, desperate to be given something new to do; others seem flattened under the weight of boredom and indifference, years upon years of it. Some are looking him up and down as though he's a piece of food they're not sure whether they'll play with, throw, or eat. Still, it's not quite as bad as the librarians' conference he spoke at last year; at least nobody's actually knitting.

Suddenly he's assailed by an image: the long supple steel of a knitting needle sliding into bruised flesh. He stops, breathes, introduces himself, waves a foxed copy of his best-known novel, *Richard and Judy* sticker faded but intact, and smiles around the room, catching everyone's eye where he can. Some don't raise their gazes to be caught; that's to be expected. There are always a few sullen ones. Their work often turns out to be the best: they've usually got something worth keeping to themselves. Although presumably everybody in this room has at least one interesting story. Except, perhaps, himself.

He drags their names out of them, then hands round a couple of extracts, popular fiction mostly: Roald Dahl, Joanna Trollope, Karin Slaughter. Keep it commercial, keep it eye-catching, easy to enjoy, easy to understand, just like his editor always says. He sits silent as a wall, one eyebrow raised encouragingly, until they trickle out some reluctant feedback. They like the Trollope best: odd, he'd thought they'd go for the darker, sharper Dahl. Then again, maybe they get enough of that in here. The word *shiv* slides into his brain and he can't yank it out. A toothbrush handle, melted over a lighter flame, whetted against bricks until it's hard and sharp as an ice-pick. He deals photos round the table like a croupier. They've been vetted for content; nothing sexy, nothing violent. A meadow, a church, a child's doll, a high-heeled shoe, a mountain, a rose, a sleeping cat, a pencil: safe things, familiar, ordinary things. Things they won't be seeing again until they get out, pencil excepted. They've all been issued with pencils for this class; the email told him no pens: presumably they're a stab-risk. Heroically, he stops himself wondering what they've all done. *Don't think, don't think.*

He realises that's he's just said this aloud.

'Don't think, don't think,' he repeats authoritatively, 'just write! That's what we're here for. Thinking only gets in the way! Right?'

'What should we write?' asks one, youngish, semi-alert, piss-blonde hair and black roots – six months since it's been dyed, he guesses. Six months inside. Her eyes are a beautiful glass-green, rimmed with red.

'Anything you like. Be free!' He winces; regroups. 'Take the photo as a starting point. A story, a poem…' This sounds weak even to him. *They're prisoners, for Christ's sake. They live by rules. They need rules. So give them some.*

'A character study,' he says. Yes. 'Think of a character inspired by the picture. They can be real, someone you know or remember – maybe a, (he glances at the church picture) a vicar you've met, or, a … florist, or someone who had a cat. Maybe you could even write about the cat?' Unexpectedly, this gets a murmur of approval. 'From the point of view, I mean, of a cat?'

Stimulated to action, his fifteen students stare with renewed interest at their deliberately banal photographs, trying to conjure something interesting from the recesses of their imaginations. He's given them twenty minutes to write something, no matter how short, and he's promised not to make them read their work aloud. Instead he'll take the pieces in, read them at home and hand them back at the next class. They don't even have to put their names on what they write if they don't want to: only a title. He insists on a title. Titles are important, he says.

He long ago gave up trying to write when his students did this exercise, because they'd all watch him, shiftily, seeing how fast he wrote and how long he paused, scoping him out, judging him, comparing their own speed and fluency of pen across paper. Normally he'd be browsing his phone under the desk at this point, but they took it off him at check-in for security reasons.

'You'd be amazed what people would do for a SIM card in here,' the humourless guard had said. 'They're like gold dust. Easy to hide, too.' She'd had plump soft hands and her nails were manicured, short and square-cut, glossy strawberry-red. For some reason this had surprised him. Unbidden, his imagination offers a number of bodily crannies where a half-inch SIM card could be concealed, and he shudders and stretches his eyes wide and concentrates on using the twenty minutes of peace he's just bought herself to observe the members of his class.

A lot of them are young; younger than he'd expected, but still old-looking, old in sin, he catches himself thinking. What is it with his brain today? Lots of Croydon facelifts and cheap bleach jobs. Lots of bad skin and frown lines, and no bloody wonder. Even this little room gives him the creeps; the institutional whitewash, the fizzing fluorescent flicker of the striplight, the high window girded by thick bars.

Most are under thirty; in for thieving and fraud and drugs offences, most likely. Three or four are forty-plus; maybe something more serious, or else repeat offences, rebounding off the cushion of normal life again and again like a snooker ball that just won't sink. (Not sure about that simile either; but it has a 1980s, cod working-class, early-Amis quality that could work; he'll examine it more closely later).

About half are black or mixed-race; he's read the stats and shouldn't be surprised, but it startles him into realising how white his classes have always been; even the outreachy, Council-sponsored ones. Surely chick-lit romance can't be a purely white phenomenon? he thinks, before realising with a horrible sort of lurch that actually, yes, it probably is: maybe not in terms of the readers, but the writers... middle-aged middle-class white folks as far as the eye can see, just like that Joanna Trollope extract. What the hell can he say to these women? What the hell will their writing say to him? And what will he say about their writing, which is almost certainly bound to be disturbing or terrible or both? Never mind: that's a problem for tomorrow, or next week, if he decides after a well-earned bottle of Merlot tonight that he's desperate enough to come back.

'Time's up!' he says brightly, thinking, but not saying, *for me anyway*. Thank God. Thank God it's over. There's something unnerving about how intensely they're all scribbling away as the little hand of the wall-clock closes in on the big, like they're racing to finish, to expel whatever it is that he's woken and is now struggling out, slowly, clumsily, eager to suck the air of freedom. He collects the papers and pencils in and stuffs them all in his bag, not looking, not counting. He doesn't notice that one of the pencils is missing.

He doesn't notice until he gets back home and takes out the crumpled, scribbled sheets and spreads them out on the dining table with Radio 3 on and a large glass of red at his side. He doesn't notice until he reaches the last story in the batch; the longest, very neatly written, in a firm small hand that gets just a little rushed and untidy on the last page, as though the writer finished it in a hurry.

His face whitens and his stomach begins to tremble as he reads. He flicks back for a name: there's nothing. He tries to remember the prisoners' faces, their hands, but they are a blur of ill-kempt anonymity. Even the title gives nothing away: the author has, with either conscious irony or a grim lack of imagination worthy of an accountancy firm, called her piece *Character Study*. Who wrote this? He has no idea. He only knows that he feels the cold, silky point of a shiv in his gut as he reads the last line:

I got the pencil: thought I'd write about you.

How did I do?

Fruit Of The Sea
Anna Fodorova

The day before the flight Julia heard on the radio that the death count had reached seven. And, that the prisoners' mothers kept a vigil in front of the jail, waiting for their sons' corpses. Then, while buttering her scone, she heard some politician's cultured voice, which he had most probably acquired during his studies abroad, assuring the journalists that the prison where the Kurdish hunger strikers were dying like flies, was one of the most modern in Europe. That was when Julia considered cancelling the holiday. But just then, Tony appeared in the door in a new pair of shorts and Julia, moved by his boyish smile and the pallor of his legs, turned the radio off.

Throughout their stay, Julia kept wondering how many more prisoners had died. But whom could she ask? Their cheerful Glaswegian representative Lorna, who kept splashing their arms with rose water while they sat cross-legged on embroidered cushions, witnessing traditional pancake making? Or the smiling waiter who greeted them with a warmth seldom offered even by the closest of one's family back home?

Tony, on the other hand, had some pressing questions of his own. Why were the stuffy twin huts in the middle of prickly brush leading to a rubbish tip described in the brochure as *spacious secluded bungalows surrounded by a fragrant Mandarin grove*; the strip of ash-coloured sand on which the restaurants spilled out its messy tables and who knows what else, *the spectacular sandy beach*? And where was the *sea* for that matter? This narrow bay of stagnant water, was *this* why they had flown across the continent?

Julia didn't mind any of that. She was happy to float in the warm, tranquil pools and stare at the yellow hills dotted with olive trees where, as Lorna has explained, Brutus had escaped from Rome after slaying Caesar. And indeed, once when Julia made Tony take a walk with her there, they stumbled over an eye glaring at them through a tuft of scorched grass, and a nostril: fragments of an ancient mosaic. In the evenings Julia liked to sit on their porch in the falling darkness, inhaling the sweet smell of bougainvillea, peeling the bitter mandarins. Once or twice she dared herself to plunge into the sea at night, to discover that parting the dark water made it alive with green fluorescent plankton that left a glowing trail on her arms.

As for Tony, it proved only a matter of days before he took to calling the sliver of grey sand *our beach*, their cramped room *our house*. He even turned a blind eye when Julia's *OTT nurturing instinct*, as he remarked to the couple from Diss next door, led her to adopt one of the scavenging cats. They fed him leftovers, which they secretly scooped from behind the waiters' backs. When the cat's scrawny body began to fill out and his face to resemble their Tabby back home (in spite of his mournful nose), they felt a glowing pride.

Their skin was turning a nice hue of gold. The days passed, punctuated by their new routine, and the nights by silent couplings – the unspoken issue being that Julia wanted a child while Tony, still young at the same age as her, didn't. In this heat their lovemaking took on a special quality and even when Tony playfully rolled over in the middle of it, staining the sheet, Julia didn't hold it against him; in fairness, she had started to monitor her fertile days recently.

One evening, in their local grocery store Julia glimpsed

on the TV a picture of police in riot gear surrounding a large building from which gaunt men were hurling bits of furniture. This was followed by a mugshot of a young man, his hair in disarray, his eyes two black targets. Luckily, Tony was in the middle of paying. When he turned, the screen flickered with explosions, the news having moved to Chechnya. 'Not a place to book a holiday, please keep it in mind,' he warned Julia. They laughed more often these days.

That night Julia hardly slept. The seafood she had ordered that evening in a sudden fling of extravagance, kept resurfacing with the urgency of an important message. When, finally, she managed to doze off, she dreamed of a huge snake, his rattling scales ablaze with bright blues, reds and greens of blinding intensity.

She woke to see Tony already dressed, loading the film into his camera. They had booked an excursion to a remote market to which the peasants brought their produce by donkey as, according to Lorna, 'they have done since time immemorial'.

Despite the early hour, the air in the room was already heavy and the moment Julia got up she felt faint. She staggered as far as their coach, her head throbbing with pain, then returned to their hut. There was no point in Tony staying behind with her; they were off home to London next day and he was looking forward to spending their every last coin in support of the local economy.

Julia passed the day oscillating between the hot lulling stillness and the choking fits that propelled her to the bathroom. Back in bed, the walls, speckled with reddish-brown smears, the minuscule mosquito memorials left by earlier holidaymakers, kept spinning around her, making her stomach swim. Finally she dozed off, losing all sense of time.

On waking she felt a presence. Expecting the reptilian greens, reds and blues, she kept her eyes shut. She could hear the rattling of its scales, faint at first, then unexpectedly, deafeningly loud. Not knowing if she was still in a dream, she looked up and saw at the door, a gaunt looking young man in a torn shirt, gasping for breath. Outside, helicopter blades sliced the air. Soon their chopping was drowned by loud voices and barking dogs.

The man stepped closer, the white bed sheet momentarily flashed in the black targets of his eyes. As the shouting and the barking approached, he put his finger to his mouth and disappeared in the bathroom, quietly closing the door behind him, and Julia wondered if she has imagined the whole thing. Then the uniforms burst in, three or four jostling in the doorway, two Alsatians pulling at the leash. Seeing the alarm on Julia's face the older man, probably an officer, ordered the dogs to be kept back.

'Prisoner ran away. No see, lady?'

Julia shook her head.

'Nice holiday, lady!'

Salutes, grins, and the door was closed.

While the police were there and also afterwards Julia, apart from that shake of her head, hadn't moved an inch; she curbed even her breath, putting herself in a trance-like state. What the fugitive's crime was, she could only guess. She hoped that he had managed to squeeze out through the skylight above the toilet.

When, a few moments later, the man materialized by her bed, shirt sticking to him, dark stubble moist with perspiration, Julia just carried on pretending to be a corpse; a corpse, unblinkingly gazing at the tree that filled the small window, each leaf sharp and bright as if lit by a spotlight. She noticed that, what she had at first taken for a shrivelled twig, was vibrating and emitting a high-pitched noise; and it occurred to her how absurd it would be if a cicada were to be the last thing she would ever see.

The hot eastern wind rushed in, blowing the muslin curtain and carrying voices, this time English. The man gasped and ducked down, just before the shadows fell in.

Julia did the last thing she'd have expected of herself, the very last thing: she reached out, her hand skimming his hair, thick and oily like plumes of a bird, and she pulled him under her sheet and covered his head, as if they were playing hide and seek.

'What a palaver! You all right in there?' The Diss couple called in.

Feeling the man's quivering form over her, lithe and angular, his sweat mingling with hers, his heart pounding against her ribs, Julia called to them that she was fine and patiently waited for them to go away. Then she did the next impossible thing: she freed one arm from under the man, then the other, and cradled his back.

Tony returned, brimming with excitement. The market was something not to be missed; he had bought a set of traditional coffee cups, and still had enough money to get Julia a present: a cotton dress ablaze with a pattern of flowers in reds, greens and blues. But when she tried it on, to Tony's disappointment it proved far too loose around her waist. Yet Julia knew he had never given her anything so fitting.

Witchburning
Richard Smyth

It's eleven at night on February sixteenth nineteen-fifty-five and the sky is lit up over Wakina Creek because the people are burning witches. One after another is thrown on the fire. They go pretty easily – they almost jump out of your arms if a breeze catches them right.

'Cold out here,' I say.

My daughter doesn't hear me. My daughter's name is Esther and she is very nearly one hundred and I fear she may be going deaf.

I repeat myself: 'Cold out here.'

She doesn't hear. She doesn't listen. I say she shouldn't be here with me, she should be over at the fire behind the pool-hall, burning witches! But she doesn't listen.

'Can't leave you here alone,' is what she says.

I'm a hundred-and-thirty-one years old and I can't be left alone. What the hell is going to happen to me that hasn't happened already, I say. She doesn't listen.

I tell her about her mother. 'it made her cry that you never gave her grandkids,' I say. She says 'you think I never cry?' Then she cries. When I feel like making Esther cry – and sometimes of course I do feel that way – I tell her about her mother.

Listen to them. I can hear them laughing from here on my front porch and they're way over there. Burning witches – tonight it seems like witchery itself. But sometimes nighttime makes you think that way.

I'll tell you about Esther's mother.

One thing about Esther's mother is that I don't recall her name. She died forty-eight years ago but Esther remembers it. She could tell you.

Bethany. Beryl. Beula, something like that, with a B.

Another thing is that she was beautiful. Now that I do remember because if every day for fifty-two years you wake up next to a beautiful woman you'll remember that she was beautiful even if you forget what she was called.

Beautiful Beula. Could've been.

What brings her to mind is that we met on February sixteenth eighteen-fifty-five, which, wait, is one hundred years ago tonight. We met at the witchburning.

I was thirty-one and I worked as a clerk for the lawyer J. Arlington Heap.

'Good evening, miss,' I say.

She doesn't say anything but she smiles. God. It was a cold night. It's always a cold night because it's always February. So you stand up close to the fire.

My brother comes over.

'Good evening, Miss Lawrence,' he says to the girl. So her second name used to be Lawrence. 'I'd like you to meet my brother, William. William, this is Miss Lawrence.'

My brother knew everybody. He worked for Macready the pharmacist and I could tell you how much use that damn Macready was but in any case Paul worked in his store and knew everybody.

Knew everything *about* everybody, too. He told me some things, hoo, you wouldn't believe them. Old Reverend deGrey had the syphilis in eighteen-sixty-nine, for one.

See – I can remember the minister's syph and I can't remember –

Betty? Belle?

Miss Lawrence, anyway, smiles at me again and I shake her hand.

'Very pleased to meet you,' I say.

'Likewise,' she says. 'You work for Mr Heap, don't you?'

'Mr *Arlington* Heap, yes,' I say. It's the kind of thing an asshole would say. Mister Arlington Heap. I was an asshole when I was thirty-one.

Paul left us alone together. Paul liked me.

We agreed, Miss Lawrence and I, that I should call on her. I called on her on a Thursday and then we got married. Why she wanted me I couldn't say. I was a legal clerk. Anybody would've done, I guess. I guess she wanted someone who could pay for her dresses et cetera – and look at me, hoo, a big-shot lawyer.

Just give me two years, five years, ten years – look at me fifty years old and still a legal clerk. Ha!

What the hell got me thinking about that?

'Cold out here,' I say.

Esther doesn't listen. As a kid she wouldn't listen. You say: 'Stay away from the creek.' She falls in the creek and breaks an arm and nearly drowns, that was when she was seven, that was, wait, eighteen-sixty-three.

I remember Gettysburg was about the same time. *Four score and seven years ago our fathers brought forth on this continent a new nation conceived in liberty.* I remember that.

I'll tell you why I was thinking about Esther's mother.

'Esther, what are you doing?' I say because now she's pouring kettle-water into the porch. Through the cracks in the porch.

'Ants,' she says. 'Little motherfuckers.' Because she's an old lady she thinks it's all right to swear like that.

I'll tell you why I was thinking about her mother.

I was thinking about the girl I knew before I met Esther's mother, two years before and I met her at the bonfire, too, which is why my train of thought – you know. This girl's name was Hilma. You want a witch to burn, here is Hilma, she's your girl.

She really was a witch. Beautiful – hoo – I couldn't tell you. You wouldn't believe it.

'Hello,' she said to me. I was walking on my own away from the fire. Paul wasn't there that year, I forget why, he wasn't there and my dad was over talking with, I recall, J. Arlington Heap.

'Good evening, ma'am.' I tipped my hat.

Hilma was a brunette which is what you'd call a *weakness* of mine. It operates on my *libido*.

'You're Billy West,' she said. Her face was pale and she stood close to me like girls didn't. Nobody ever called me Billy, not that I minded it, I liked it, 'Billy', but to everyone I was William.

'I am.'

'Billy the lawyer.'

'Hell of a lawyer.'

She laughed because she knew I was just a legal clerk.

Hilma took me by the hand and led me away from the fire. I didn't know what the hell was going on and I wasn't thinking about much. Probably I was thinking about my twenty-nine-year-old woody, never been used, one careful owner, ha.

She took me into the trees. The trees were wet and black.

Before I get involved in it the story of it is this: in sixteen-forty-nine Judge Christopher Wrecsam burned his first witch on the night of February sixteenth in the town of Wakina Creek. He didn't stop until he died of tuberculosis in sixteen-fifty-eight.

I remember, they said in school, the first witch Judge

Wrecsam burned was a schoolmistress named Mary Quincey.

Ever since then Wakina Creek builds a bonfire and burns witches all night on February sixteenth, until sunrise of the seventeenth. Why the hell stop on the seventeenth, Wrecsam didn't, why not carry right on, eighteenth nineteenth twentieth, February March April right through spring summer winter, burn yourselves a witch every fucking day.

She took me into the trees. She took me to a clearing in the trees.

'Do you want to know a secret?' she says – hoo, the secrets she knew.

'Sure.'

'Are you *really* sure?' this girl Hilma says. We're in this clearing. I can hear people around the fire talking and laughing and shouting and so on and I can hear the fire crackle.

Here it's cold and here it's dark. I remember. Strange, to hear the fire and still be in darkness.

Hilma kissed me. *That* I remember. My first time. Twenty-nine damned years old.

'Are you really sure?' She repeats herself.

'Yes.'

Hilma was a witch, indeed, and I fell in love with her. I didn't have a choice – I don't know, do you ever? It wasn't witchery, is what I mean. Not then, she didn't have to do witchcraft to make me fall in love with her. All she had to do was take off my pants and jump me.

Don't tell me I'm not a romantic, no, I won't have that. I was a romantic, crazy, look at me: twenty-nine, a legal clerk to a deadend lawyer, in the woods in February, naked as a baby with this beautiful girl – I don't have to draw a picture, you know what screwing looks like.

Crazy.

When we were finished, she goes: 'Do you love me?' and I go: 'Yes.'

'Watch,' she says.

She lifts her white arms and her black hair is falling over her breasts and she lifts herself three feet off the ground. The dead leaves circle her feet like in a twister.

'Watch,' she says.

She writes in the air with her finger: *Hilma* and then *love*. She says: 'Watch'.

She moves her arm and there's silence. I mean silence. I can't hear the people round the witchburning fire and I can't hear anything. Again she kisses me, this witch, the witch and the legal clerk who loved her. It's a joke! Ha.

Afterwards I walked back to the fire. I don't know where Hilma went. I know that in the spring her family moved back to Appalachia where they came from.

Bess, Bessie? No. You shall have to ask Esther who remembers.

'Cold out here,' I say. I expect I'll die of the cold tonight. Ironic, is what you call it, when the witches, two-hundred witches die in the flames and I die of the cold.

William West, died of the cold nineteen-fifty-five. William West, burned as a witch.

Don't think they don't say it. I am a hundred-and-thirty-one years old and people don't like it. I've heard them say that Esther's a witch. I've heard them say she keeps me alive by witchcraft. In this day and age I don't believe it. In this day and age, the *nuclear* age. Who the hell needs witchcraft?

'You want a blanket out here, it's cold,' says Esther.

'I hadn't noticed,' I say.

'I've got a fire on inside. There's a fire going,' she says. She goes back inside to where it's warm.

I don't know. Tonight the witchburning seems like witchery itself. I threw witches on the fire myself when I was young and I can still remember the way they felt against my skin and how they made me itch – I don't know, doesn't it mean that if you remember how it felt somehow you still feel it?

I'm a hundred-and-thirty-one and I don't feel much. Particularly in this cold and she hasn't brought me a blanket, she's forgotten. I expect I shall die, only –

The thing is I don't want to freeze with tears in my eyes.

Esther gets the fire going with paper dollies. She takes the *South Bend Eagle* and takes each page and twists it into a little newspaper dolly and sets it in the fire. I know, I've seen her do it. Is she going crazy? She's always done it. I think she did it when she was a little girl.

She's been burning little witches all these years but then who the hell hasn't?

When I married Esther's mother I burned a witch and I'm burning witches all of the time pretty much. How did I get on to thinking like this? I suppose – well, you try thinking for a hundred-and-thirty-one years and see if there's any damn thing you don't start thinking about.

'You coming in? You better come in,' Esther says. I suppose she's all right. Anyway she helps me up out of my chair and takes my cold hands and the big bonfire's still flaming away behind the pool-hall.

We go in. She's poured me a glass of whisky and I know if I drink it I'll tell Esther about her mother and make her cry. But maybe instead I'll tell her how I always loved her mother, and how her mother always loved her, and how I love her, ah hell yes, and how, and how –

But I can see the little paper dollies burning up in the fire and I don't want to burn any more witches. I'll drink the damn whisky and I'll make her cry.

Inscription on reverse of this photographic plate.
This Daguerreotype was taken Aug. 1845. It is a copy of Captain Jonathan Walker's hand as branded by the U.S. Marshall of the Dist. of Florida for having helped 7 men to obtain 'Life Liberty, and Happiness.' SS Slave Saviour Northern Dist. SS Slave Stealer Southern Dist.

The Branded Hand
Brian Johnstone

They printed this in Florida,
a slave state still in forty-five,
its marshal with the power
to mark a man for life. Yet,

he can't have lived for long
till someone in New England
passed comment on his scars,
desired that he submit again

to steel that clamped the arm
lest movement spoil a plate
and new technology distort
the marks that he displayed,

his palm extended, opened
to their lens. As it had been
to coals, to branding irons,
the double *S* that found him,

in The South, slave stealer,
thief of someone's property
he only saw as fellow men
in need. But, in The North,

a saviour offering the chance
for freedom crossing borders
meant to those who'd borne
the scars or more themselves

in multitudes, unrecorded,
never photographed, but
fixed, as is this single print,
in time, a record of its hand.

Et statim post pacis reformacionem amovebimus de regno omnes alienigenas milites, balistarios, servientes, stipendiarios, qui venerint cum equis et armis ad nocumentum regni.

As soon as peace is restored, we will remove from the kingdom all the foreign knights, bowmen, their attendants, and the mercenaries that have come to it, to its harm, with horses and arms

Black & White
Brian Johnstone
From a photograph of Nazi troops in occupied Crete.

It's what they might be saying in casual conversation
chills the blood. Only one man eyes the camera; while
others glance at Cretans stepping past them in the street
with what, to read the faces in the photograph, is contempt.

The bulk, backs turned away, engage with comrades,
heads inclined to listen, while, here and there, a smile
is on a face. All chatting, maybe talking of their homes,
outside this requisitioned *kafenion* signed in Gothic script.

Each character is brutal, a black and white assertion
of command; each one a signal of the future this village
can expect, its fate to be reluctant host to the *Soldatenheim*,
a home from home for those at once detested and opposed.

The thoughts these men in summer uniform – shorts
to combat drowsy heat – exchanged there in the street
are lost. As were all of fighting age in village after village,
shot upon the ridge inscribed with names in black and white.

And in amongst the widows' houses, few left whole,
was thrust this *soldiers' home*, inciting hatred and defiance
in the Cretans passing by, eyes fixed dead ahead with what,
to read the faces in the print, is much more than just contempt.

Liceat unicuique decetero exire de regno nostro, et redire,
salvo et secure, per terram et per aquam, salva fide
nostra, nisi tempore gwerre per aliquod breve tempus,
propter communem utilitatem regni

In future it shall be lawful for any man to leave
and return to our kingdom unharmed and without
fear, by land or water, preserving his allegiance to
us, except in time of war, for some short period, for
the common benefit of the realm.

The Privilege of Departure
or Dover-bound but Delayed
Bernie Howley

Packed to bursting a people carrier   plus top box
rumbles up the ramp and rolls to a halt in a designated bay
doors fly open.

A crude bass line
   kiddy-babble
         shrill instructions
               a curse a whine
                       fall
onto the car deck to mingle
with echo-y engine thrums
and a tinny Tannoy heckle that warns foot passengers
again   and again   and again
to watch out for moving vehicles

The disgorging hordes drift upward
to cafés and bars upper decks window seats rail-side spots
to watch the land mass diminish to a dismal smudge
to complain at the delay
Queues are long on board ten minutes to get
an insipid coffee sub-standard sandwich a cake
of cardboard texture
and dietary dissent subverts a frail
must-enjoy-every-last-minute
mania

Peacemaker types pull phones from pockets
click on holiday snaps flick them back and forth
tilt and tip them for portrait for landscape for the best effect
to distract the disgruntled diners

A determined few persist
in chewing over their particular miseries
and talk turns to pernickety bosses
                        and the tedium of employment
to first days of the new school year
                    and teachers with imagined grudges.
A couple pore over a pile of receipts reminders
of overindulgences only ever condoned in Euros
and they panic

A cat is fretted over   shrilly
how will it have been   for her, two weeks in a cattery?
She'll have to do an extra night now.
Mum engages with the horizon and sniffs
Dad bemoans the added outlay
their ten year-old mumbles get a grip
his eyes fixed on his smartphone

The call comes for a return to the car decks
A swarm of beings tanned and dishevelled speeds
to arrive as one at narrow portals en route to the ship's bowels.
Eye contact stops
                Shoulders dip
                        and the rush is on
because being the first to one's car
                                matters?

Omnes autem istas consuetudines predictas et libertates quas nos concessimus in regno nostro tenendas quantum ad nos pertinet erga nostros, omnes de regno nostro, tam clerici quam laici, observent quantum ad se pertinet erga suos.

Cum autem pro Deo, et ad emendacionem regni nostri, et ad melius sopiendum discordiam inter nos et barones nostros ortam, hec omnia predicta concesserimus, volentes ea integra et firma stabilitate in perpetuum gaudere, facimus et concedimus eis securitatem subscriptam;

si nos, vel justiciarius noster, vel ballivi nostri, vel aliquis de ministris nostris, in aliquo erga aliquem deliquerimus, vel aliquem articulorum pacis aut securitatis transgressi fuerimus, et delictum ostensum fuerit accedant ad nos proponentes nobis excessum; petent ut excessum illum sine dilacione faciamus emendari.

Et si nos excessum non emendaverimus, vel, si nos non emendaverit infra tempus quadraginta dierum, illi cum communia tocius terre distringent et gravabunt nos modis omnibus quibus poterunt, scilicet per capcionem castrorum, terrarum, possessionum, et aliis modis quibus poterunt, donec fuerit emendatum secundum arbitrium eorum, salva persona nostra et regine nostre et liberorum nostrorum; et cum fuerit emendatum intendent nobis sicut prius fecerunt.

Data per manum nostram in prato quod vocatur Ronimed, inter Windlesoram et Stanes, quinto decimo die junii, anno regni nostri decimo septimo.

All these customs and liberties that we have granted shall be observed in our kingdom in so far as concerns our own relations with our subjects. Let all men of our kingdom, whether clergy or laymen, observe them similarly in their relations with their own men.

Since we have granted all these things for God, for the better ordering of our kingdom, and to allay the discord that has arisen between us and our barons, and since we desire that they shall be enjoyed in their entirety, with lasting strength, for ever, we give and grant to the barons the following security:

If we, our chief justice, our officials, or any of our servants offend in any respect against any man, or transgress any of the articles of the peace or of this security, and the offence is made known, they shall come to us - to declare it and claim immediate redress.

If we make no redress within forty days, they may distrain upon and assail us in every way possible, with the support of the whole community of the land, by seizing our castles, lands, possessions, or anything else saving only our own person and those of the queen and our children, until they have secured such redress as they have determined upon. Having secured the redress, they may then resume their normal obedience to us.

Given by our hand in the meadow that is called Runnymede, between Windsor and Staines, on the fifteenth day of June in the seventeenth year of our reign.

ABOUT THE AUTHORS

Alison Lock's poetry and short stories have appeared in anthologies and journals in the UK and internationally, Her first poetry collection, *A Slither of Air*, was winner of the Indigo Dreams Poetry Collection Competition 2010; her second, *Beyond Wings*, published 2015. She is the author of a short story collection, and a fantasy novel, *Maysun and the Wingfish* (Mother's Milk Books 2016) She has an MA in Literature Studies and is a tutor for courses on Transformative Life Writing.

Andrew McCallum lives and works in Lowland Scotland. He writes in both Scots and English, and his poetry has been broadcast and published widely in Britain and North America. Poems have appeared in dozens of anthologies and in magazines and journals too numerous to list.

Anna Fodorova has made TV animation films, written TV film scripts, worked as lecturer in art colleges, and is now in private practice as a psychotherapist.

Her children's book, *Carlo the Crocodile*, was published by A.C. Black, and her novel *The Training Patient*, and a story included in *Tales of Psychotherapy*, were published by Karnac. Anna also has a story in Arachne's *Stations*.

Bernie Howley is a Bath-based writer, poet and workshop leader. After working as a research scientist, teacher and homemaker she came to writing, creatively, only recently. To get up to speed she went back to education and picked up a BA in Creative Writing and an MA in Writing For Young People from Bath Spa University. It has been fun and life changing.

Brian Johnstone's work has appeared throughout Scotland, in the UK, North America and Europe. He has published six collections, his latest being *Dry Stone Work* (Arc, 2014). He has read at various international poetry festivals from Macedonia to Nicaragua, and at venues across the UK. Later in 2014 his work will be appearing on The Poetry Archive website.

His poem *Robinson* appeared in Arachne's *The Other Side of Sleep*. *A Black and White Print* was inspired by a photograph found in a book, which we have been completely unable to trace. Website: http://brianjohnstonepoet.co.uk

Carolyn Eden has had a number of short stories read at Liars' League London and Hong Kong. Her poem *Promotional Samples* was performed at Arachne Press's *Liberty Tales* event, and is reimagined here as a story. Her story *Late Night* was published online in *.Cent Magazine*. Carolyn is currently writing a novel and a collection of poetry entitled *It's Not About Me*. Her alter-ego, Carrie Cohen, is an actress who regularly narrates stories for various groups; last year's highlight was reading at the Serpentine Gallery. Her hobbies are all things literary, theatre, discussing politics, eating and dieting. She is better at the penultimate pastime than the last.

Cassandra Passarelli A vagrant at heart, Cassandra has spent much time wandering, from Guatemala to Burma, between the tropics of Cancer and Capricorn. She's published a couple of dozen stories and been short-listed for literary prizes. She lives in East Devon with her daughter.

Cherry Potts is the author of a novel, *The Dowry Blade*, two collections of short stories, and many stories in anthologies and magazines. She runs Arachne Press, and edits anthologies including Award Winning *Weird Lies*. She runs live lit event *The Story Sessions*, and literature & music festival *Solstice Shorts*.

David Guy (@TedVaak) is the writer of a number of picture books for children, including *The Saddest Bear Of All*, *Do Not Disturb The Dragon* and *Spiders Are Wonderful*. He used to write and edit the science fiction, horror and folklore magazine *Essex Terror*. Some of his work can be found here: https://medium.com/

For 35 years **David Mathews** was a work psychologist, winkling out other people's stories, you might say. Originally from Wales, he lives in Bath and SW France. He has had short stories published in magazines and anthologies, including *Wednesday Afternoon* in *Solstice Shorts: Sixteen Stories about Time.* David also features in the second Solstice Shorts Festival, Longest Night, and his story, *Mouse*, will be in the *Shortest Day, Longest Night* anthology, which will be published in November 2016. His characters from Border Country, Buck, Rhys and Lewis, also feature in his 2016 charity publication, *A Baker's Dozen: Thirteen stories about scones.*

Elinor Brooks grew up in Edinburgh and now lives in Wiltshire where, until recently, she taught English and Creative Writing. Her poems have appeared on the big screen, on fridge magnets and even on an adshel. Most recently she has been published in *The Listening Walk* (Bath Poetry Café Anthology) and online at *And Other Poems* ed. Josephine Corcoran. In 2015 her poem *The Oxford Girl* was shortlisted in the Poetry Kit summer competition, *Cities.*

Helen Morris @mortaltaste lives and works in Essex. She tries to fit in writing stories between doing the washing for three sons, swimming too much, eating delicious food and drinking good beer. Poppies was inspired by a photograph at http://www.theleevalley.co.uk/programme/land-girls.html.

Jeremy Dixon was born in Essex and now lives in rural South Wales making Artist's Books that combine poetry and photography. His poems have appeared both online and in print. For more information please visit www.hazardpress. co.uk, or follow him on Twitter @HazardPressUK.

Jim Cogan is a writer, filmmaker and occasional cartoonist of diverse Northern stock, currently based in Oxfordshire. Several of his stories have been read at Liars' League including *Lag, Memory Man, The Baggage Handlers* and *33,333rd Time Lucky.*

Kate Foley is a widely published, prize-winning poet who has read in many UK and European locations. Her first collection, *Soft Engineering* was short listed for best first collection at Aldeburgh. She lives with her wife, between Amsterdam and Suffolk, where she performs, writes, edits, leads workshops and whenever possible works with artists in other disciplines. Her poem *The Other Side of Sleep,* the title poem for Arachne Press' first poetry anthology, won the 2014 *Second Light* Long Poem competition, and her eighth collection *The Don't Touch Garden* was also published by Arachne Press.

Katy Darby co-runs Liars' League and teaches Short Story Writing and Writers' Workshop at City University, London. Her first novel, *The Whores' Asylum*, aka *The Unpierced Heart*, is published by Penguin. Katy is the co-editor of *London Lies, Lovers' Lies* and *Weird Lies*.

Liam Hogan is a London based writer and host of the award winning monthly literary event, Liars' League. Winner of Quantum Shorts 2015 and the Sci-Fest LA's Roswell Award 2016, he's been published in anthologies *London Lies* (Arachne Press), *Wax&Wane* (NoseTouch Press), *Beware the Little White Rabbit* (Leap Books) and online at DailyScienceFiction and NoSleep Podcast. Liam's first collection of stories, *Happy Ending NOT Guaranteed* will be published by Arachne Press in 2017. Find out more at http://happyendingnotguaranteed.blogspot.co.uk/

Nick Rawlinson is an actor and audiobook reader. His work has been shortlisted for the Bristol Prize (twice) and made the longlist for the Sean O'Faolain Prize.

Owen Townend is primarily a writer of short speculative fiction because 'life makes such beautiful oddities'. He attended the MA Writing degree at Sheffield Hallam University and currently daylights in libraries. He is on Twitter @mrpondersome and has a blog http://mrpondersome.blogspot.co.uk/.

Peter DeVille writes poetry and prose and has been published widely in British, other European and American magazines and in anthologies and Internet magazines. He also writes literary reviews. Two collections of his poems, *Open Eye* and *Taking the pH* are published by Tuba Press UK www.tubapress.eu and *25 poems Ciao Marco Martial*, inspired by reading the Latin poet, by Shoestring Press UK. He has been awarded a Fellowship in poetry of the Hawthornden Foundation UK/USA and a Fellowship in literature of the Bogliasco Foundation Italy/USA.

Richard Smyth is a freelance writer. He has published two non-fiction books: *Bumfodder* (Souvenir Press, 2012) and *Bloody British History: Leeds* (The History Press, 2013) and has had short fiction published in *The Stinging Fly, The Fiction Desk, .Cent, Vintage Script* and a *Spilling Ink* anthology.

Sarah Evans has had over a hundred stories published in anthologies, magazines and online. Prizes have been awarded by, amongst others: Words and Women, Winston Fletcher, Stratford Literary Festival, Glass Woman and Rubery. Other publishing outlets include: the Bridport Prize, Unthank Books, Bloomsbury and Best New Writing. She has also had work performed in London, Hong Kong and New York.

MORE FROM ARACHNE PRESS
www.arachnepress.com

BOOKS

COMING SOON:

Shortest Day, Longest Night
ISBN: 978-1-909208-28-5
Stories and poems from the *Solstice Shorts Festival* 2015 and 2016.

With Paper for Feet by Jennifer A. McGowan
ISBN: 978-1-909208-35-3
Narrative poems based in myth and folk stories from around the world.

Happy Ending NOT Guaranteed by Liam Hogan
ISBN: 978-1-909208-36-0
Deliciously twisted fantasy stories.

BACK LIST*:*

Short Stories

London Lies
ISBN: 978-1-909208-00-1
Our first Liars' League showcase, featuring unlikely tales set in London.

Stations: Short Stories Inspired by the Overground line
ISBN: 978-1-909208-01-8
A story for every station from New Cross, Crystal Palace, and West Croydon at the Southern extremes of the East London branch of the Overground line, all the way to Highbury & Islington.

Lovers' Lies
ISBN: 978-1-909208-02-5
Our second collaboration with Liars' League, bringing the freshness, wit, imagination and passion of their authors to stories of love.

Weird Lies
ISBN: 978-1-909208-10-0
WINNER of the Saboteur2014 Best Anthology Award: our third Liars' League collaboration – more than twenty stories varying in style from tales not out of place in *One Thousand and One Nights* to the completely bemusing.

Solstice Shorts: Sixteen Stories about Time
ISBN: 978-1-909208-23-0
Winning stories from the first *Solstice Shorts Festival* competition together with a story from each of the competition judges.

Mosaic of Air, Cherry Potts
ISBN: 978-1-909208-03-2
Sixteen short stories from a lesbian perspective.

Poetry
The Other Side of Sleep: Narrative Poems
ISBN: 978-1-909208-18-6
Long, narrative poems by contemporary voices, including Inua Elams, Brian Johnstone, and Kate Foley, whose title poem for the anthology was the winner of the 2014 *Second Light* Long Poem competition.

The Don't Touch Garden, Kate Foley
ISBN: 978-1-909208-19-3
A complex autobiographical collection of poems of adoption and identity, from award-winning poet Kate Foley.

Novels

Devilskein & Dearlove, Alex Smith
ISBN: 978-1-909208-15-5
NOMINATED FOR THE 2015 CILIP CARNEGIE MEDAL.
A young adult novel set in South Africa. Young Erin Dearlove
has lost everything, and is living in a run-down apartment block
in Cape Town. Then she has tea with Mr Devilskein, the demon
who lives on the top floor, and opens a door into another world.

The Dowry Blade, Cherry Potts
ISBN: 979-1-909208-20-9
When nomad Brede finds a wounded mercenary and the Dowry
Blade, she is set on a journey of revenge, love, and loss.

Photography

Outcome: LGBT Portraits
ISBN: 978-1-909208-26-1
80 full colour photographic portraits of LGBT people with the
attributes of their daily life - and a photograph of themselves as
a child.

All our books (except *The Other Side of Sleep* and *The Don't
Touch Garden)* are also available as e-books.

EVENTS

Arachne Press is enthusiastic about live literature and we make an effort to present our books through readings.

The Solstice Shorts Festival

(http://arachnepress.com/solstice-shorts)

Solstice Shorts is our first experiment in running an all-day event, we hope there will be many more.

We showcase our work and that of others at our own bi-monthly live literature event, in south London: *The Story Sessions* which we run like a folk club, with headliners and opportunities for the audience to join in (http://arachnepress. com/the-story-sessions)

We are always on the lookout for other places to show off, so if you run a bookshop, a literature festival or any other kind of literature venue, get in touch; we'd love to talk to you.

WORKSHOPS

We offer writing workshops suitable for writers' groups, literature festivals, evening classes, which are sometimes supported by live music – if you are interested, please get in touch.